# THE GOLD JEWELRY BUYING GUIDE

Text & Photographs

by

**RENEE NEWMAN**

**International Jewelry Publications**

Los Angeles

This publication is designed to provide information in regard to the subject matter covered. It is sold with the understanding that the publisher and author are not engaged in rendering legal, financial, or other professional services. If legal or other expert assistance is required, the services of a competent professional should be sought. International Jewelry Publications and the author shall have neither liability nor responsibility to any person or entity with respect to any loss or damage caused or alleged to be caused directly or indirectly by the information contained in this book. All inquiries should be directed to:

**International Jewelry Publications**
P.O. Box 13384
Los Angeles, CA 90013-0384 USA


(Inquiries should be accompanied by a self-addressed, stamped envelope).



Printed in Singapore

10   9   8   7   6   5   4   3   2   1



**Library of Congress Cataloging in Publication Data**

Newman, Renée.
    The gold jewelry buying guide / text & photographs by Renée Newman.
        p.  cm.
    Includes bibliographical references and index.
    ISBN 0-929975-19-7 : $19.95
    1. Gold Jewelry--Purchasing. I. Title.
TS729.N48   1993
739.27--dc20                                   93-17583
                                                  CIP

**Cover photograph** by
Renée Newman
The 14K pin/pendant and gold chain is courtesy of
Gregory Mikaelian & Sons Inc., Los Angeles, CA
Wax sculpture and design by Peggy Croft

# Contents

# Contents

# Preface

How can someone who's not a jeweler write a valid book about gold jewelry?

This is a logical question for readers to ask. Although I've taken many jewelry-related courses, I'm not qualified to make or repair jewelry. I'm a gemologist by training, and I'm much more skilled at evaluating diamonds than gold mountings. However, one of my responsibilities has been jewelry quality control, and this is what aroused my interest in jewelry craftsmanship.

Realizing that experienced jewelers are the best source of information on gold jewelry, I interviewed more than 200 of them. Although they were from various cities throughout North America, many were born and/or trained abroad. I asked them open-ended questions such as "What types of gold chains do you recommend?...What craftsmanship problems have you found with jewelry brought in for repair?...How can a layperson tell if a jewelry piece is of good quality?...What advice would you give consumers about buying gold jewelry?"

I also talked to gold assayers, appraisers, gold-chain importers, pawn brokers, coin dealers, and friends & relatives who had had both good and bad experiences buying jewelry. To better understand the customer's perspective, I went into stores and pretended I wanted to buy some gold jewelry. In addition, I found valuable data in the reference materials cited in the bibliography of this book. The result of my research is *The Gold Jewelry Buying Guide*.

With regard to the state of jewelry craftsmanship today, my survey of jewelers revealed three basic viewpoints: A few jewelers said there *was* no problem with jewelry quality. According to them, the only problem is that people abuse their jewelry. As one jeweler succinctly put it, "Chains will break, stones will fall out, and prongs will wear out just like the soles of your shoes. It's only normal."

9

Another group of jewelers believes that a lot of jewelry sold today is not well-made, but it would hurt the industry if consumers knew this. In fact, one jeweler felt the decline in craftsmanship had *benefitted* the public and the industry. He reasoned that lowered quality has allowed jewelry prices to drop, and this, in turn, has increased sales and boosted the economy.

The majority of jewelers acknowledged a decline in jewelry quality and felt the public should be informed about craftsmanship. According to them, increased knowledge leads to better buying choices. And when customers are happy with their jewelry purchases, they are likely to buy and spend more.

In addition to the decline in workmanship, jewelers were concerned about unethical trade practices. Some of those most frequently mentioned were:

♦ Rhodium plating yellow gold and calling it white gold.

♦ Making, sizing and repairing 14K and 18K gold jewelry with silver, lead, or lower-karat gold solder.

♦ Making, sizing and repairing platinum jewelry with white gold and white gold solder without the customer's permission.

♦ Phony discounts and going out of business sales.

Underkarated jewelry (containing less gold than marked) was not often mentioned by jewelers. However, people who have reason to test their gold or get it assayed (e.g. gold buyers) claim it is a major problem.

Besides providing me with a lot of information, jewelers have contributed photos or have given me jewelry to photograph. Some have read over portions of the book, and their recommendations have resulted in important changes and additions to the text.

Many of the jewelers I worked with told me they were delighted they could help me with my research. They want information on craftsmanship made available to the public. It is their desire that consumers not only get good value for their money but that they also get a lot of pleasure from buying and owning jewelry. That's what I hope you'll learn by reading *The Gold Jewelry Buying Guide*.

# Acknowledgements

I would like to express my appreciation to the following people for their contribution to *The Gold Jewelry Buying Guide*:

Ernie and Regina Goldberger of the Josam Diamond Trading Corporation. This book could never have been written without the experience and knowledge I gained from working with them.

Erik Anderson, Martin Bell, Mark Castagnoli, Carl Denney, Les DeVito, Mark Fischer, Mitch Forest, Skip Gunter, Scott Hallock, Louise Harris, Alan Hodgkinson, Howard Horowitz, Richard Kimball, Jonathan Locke, Peter Malnekoff, Steve Mikaelian, Michael Quigley, Steve Page, Debra Petres, Alan Revere, Louise B. Stein, Dale Swanson. They have made valuable suggestions, corrections, and comments regarding the portions of the book they examined. They are not responsible for any possible errors, nor do they necessarily endorse the material contained in this book.

A & A Findings, Aurora Imports Inc., Benjamin & Co., Peggy Croft, Patricia Esparza, Mark Fischer, Hallock Jewelry, Inc., Josam Diamond Trading Corp, Jane Keller, Eva Kemper, Kevorks Jewelry, Garbis Mazmanian, Media Imports, Inc., Gregory Mikaelian & Sons Inc., William and Linda Newton, Jane Nordvedt, Alan Revere, Timeless Gem Designs, Sandra Weaver, and Nerses Yahiayan. Jewelry, chains, and/or related materials from them were used in some of the photographs.

Asian Institute of Gemological Sciences, Maurice Badler Fine Jewelry, Canadian Placer Gold, Ltd., Peggy Croft, Erik Jewelers, Forest Jewelers, Global Diamonds Inc., H H Gold. Inc., Hallock Coin Jewelry, Alan Hodgkinson, Gemological Institute of America, Richard Kimball, Hans Kober, Landstrom's, Levine Designs, Alan Revere, River Gems and Findings, The Roxx Limited, Stamper Black Hills Gold Jewelry, South Dakota Gold Co., Tri-Electronics, Inc., Wideband Jewelry Corp. Photos or diagrams from them have been reproduced in this book.

Robert Adem, Michael Elliott, Jim Rich, and Leo Schmied. Besides providing information on gold testing, they also gave practical demonstrations.

All the jewelers and gold dealers who have helped me with my research. They are too numerous to be mentioned.

Ion Itescu, J. C. Lim, and Lisa Tse. They have provided technical assistance.

Patricia S. Esparza. She has spent hours carefully editing *The Gold Jewelry Buying Guide*. Thanks to her, this book is much easier for consumers to read and understand.

My sincere thanks to all of these contributors for their kindness and help.

# Suppliers of Jewelry for Photographs

**Cover Photo:** Gregory Mikaelian & Sons, Inc., Los Angeles, CA, designed by Peggy Croft

**Color Photos:**

Pages 49-56

3a  Maurice Badler Fine Jewelry, New York, NY
3b  Timeless Gem Designs, Los Angeles, CA
3c  Richard Kimball, Denver, CO
3d  William Newton, San Francisco, CA
4a & b  Peggy Croft Wax Sculpting, Los Angeles, CA
4c  Maurice Badler Fine Jewelry, New York, NY
4d  Mark Fischer, Dreams of Gold, Inc., South Bend, IN
4e  Alan Revere Jewelry Design, San Francisco, CA
4f  The Roxx Limited, Baltimore, MD
4g  Asian Institute of Gemological Sciences (AIGS), Bangkok, Thailand
10a  Media Imports Inc., Los Angeles, CA
5a & b  Forest Jewelers, Princeton, NJ
5c  Gregory Mikaelian & Sons, Inc., Los Angeles, CA
5d  Erik Jewelers, Buffalo, NY

Pages 139-144

10b & c  made by Bert McCrum, designed by Alan Hodgkinson, Clarkston, Glasgow, Scotland
10d  Global Diamonds, Inc., made and designed by Dean Moy, Chicago, IL
10e  Richard Kimball, Denver, CO
10f  South Dakota Gold, Rapid City, SD
10g  Landstrom's, Rapid City, SD
10h & i  Stamper Black Hills Gold Jewelry, Rapid City, SD
11a & d  Wideband Jewelry Corp, New Rochelle, NY
11b  Hallock Coin Jewelry, Anaheim, CA
11c & e  HH Gold, Inc., Tarzana, CA

## Black & White Photos

### Chapter 3

Fig. 3.3  Just for Fun Cohen Co., Doraville, Georgia
Fig. 3.6  Levine Design, Pittsburgh, PA
Fig. 3.7  Richard Kimball, Denver, CO
FIg. 3.8  Canadian Placer Gold Ltd., Vancouver, British Columbia

### Chapter 4

Figs. 4.1 & 4.2  Nerses Yahiayan, Los Angeles, CA
Fig. 4.3  Stamper Black Hills Gold Jewelry, Rapid City, SD
Fig. 4.4  Erik Jewelers, Buffalo, NY
Fig. 4.5  A & A Findings, Los Angeles, CA
Fig. 4.6  Maurice Badler Fine Jewelry, New York, NY
Fig. 4.7  Alan Revere Jewelry Design, San Francisco, CA
Fig. 4.8  The Roxx Limited, Baltimore, MD

### Chapter 5

Fig. 5.2  Kevork's Jewelry, Los Angeles, CA
Fig. 5.3  Mazman Jewelry, Los Angeles, CA
Fig. 5.4  River Gems & Findings, Albuquerque, NM
Fig. 5.11  Forest Jewelers, Princeton, NJ

### Chapter 6

Fig. 6.1  A & A Findings, Los Angeles, CA
Fig. 6.12  Levine Design, Pittsburgh, PA
Fig. 6.16  Mazman Jewelry, Los Angeles, CA
Fig. 6.17  Josam Diamond Trading Corporation, Los Angeles, CA
Fig. 6.18  Richard Kimball, Denver, CO

### Chapter 7

Figs. 7.1 & 2  Benjamin & Co., Los Angeles, CA
Fig. 7.3  Hallock Jewelry, Anaheim, CA
Fig. 7.4 & 7.7,  Media Imports, Los Angeles, CA
Fig. 7.9  Aurora Imports Inc., Los Angeles, CA
Fig. 7.10  Benjamin & Co., Los Angeles, CA
Fig. 7.11-12, 7.14-15  Media Imports, Los Angeles, CA
Fig. 7.16  Benjamin & Co., Los Angeles, CA
Fig. 7.18  (chain)  Aurora Imports Inc., Los Angeles, CA

**Chapter 9**

Fig. 9.1  Tri Electronics Inc, San Diego, CA

**Chapter 10**

Fig. 10.1  Landstrom's, Rapid City, SD
Fig. 10.2  Stamper Black Hills Gold Jewelry, Rapid City, SD
Fig. 10.3  South Dakota Gold, Rapid City, SD

**Chapter 11**

Fig. 11.1  HH Gold Inc., Tarzana, CA
Fig. 11.2  Wideband Jewelry Corp., New Rochelle, NY
Fig. 11.3  Hallock Coin Jewelry., Anaheim, CA
Fig. 11.4  Wideband Jewelry Corp., New Rochelle, NY
Fig. 11.5  HH Gold Inc., Tarzana, CA
Figs. 11.6-10  Wideband Jewelry Corp., New Rochelle, NY

**Chapter 14**

Fig. 14.1  Made by Bert McCrum, designed by Alan Hodgkinson, Clarkston, Glasgow, Scotland

# 1

# Why Read a Whole Book Just to Buy Gold Jewelry?

```
GOLD CHAINS  80% OFF
```

This sign caught Ruth's eye. She needed a chain, but didn't want to pay full price. This was the highest discount she'd seen anywhere, so she decided to have a look at the chains. The chain she liked best was a bit wider than she wanted, but she bought it anyway. Ruth wasn't going to pass up a deal like this one.

While browsing in another jewelry store, she saw a chain like hers for a little less. She asked the owner, Eldon, what the difference was between the two chains. He checked and found they were both the same width, length, and style. They were both 14K and had the same trademark. The only difference was that Eldon's weighed about 3/10 of a gram more.

Ruth was puzzled. Eldon's chain was the same as hers but a bit lower priced. Yet he didn't display any discount signs. She asked him why.

He replied. "I have a regular clientele that knows I charge fair prices and offer good quality and service. They'd be insulted if I hiked up my price 500% and then offered a phony 80% discount. I teach my customers how to compare quality and prices, not percentage discounts."

Nancy and John were in a jewelry store looking at engagement rings. After browsing for awhile, Nancy spotted an unusual ring with a marquise diamond. She wanted a ring with style and this one had it, so she asked the salesperson if she could try it on. The ring fit perfectly. It was striking, yet dainty. Both John and Nancy agreed that they should get this ring, so they did.

A year after their wedding, Nancy was handwashing some wool sweaters. When she was finished, she noticed the diamond in her engagement ring was missing. She looked in the sink and through her sweaters, but couldn't find it. The diamond she had hoped would last forever was forever gone.

Jean was at the local flea market looking for a gold bangle bracelet. The prices of one vendor, named Tony, were a lot lower than his competitors around him. When Jean asked why, Tony explained that his gold jewelry was made at his family's factory in Italy. Since there were no middlemen involved, he was able to sell his goods for less.

Jean found a bracelet she liked for just $110. It was solid and very wide. She had heard that if there was a trademark next to the karat stamp of a piece, that meant it was real gold. This bracelet was marked 14K and had a trademark, so she bought it.

After Jean had worn it for a few months, she noticed some dark spots on the bracelet. She couldn't clean them off, so she took the bracelet to a jeweler and asked him what the problem was. He looked at it and told her the bracelet was plated, and some of the gold plating had worn off.

Bob turned on the TV. A lady was selling a gold necklace.

> "I'm really going to stun you today. In my hand is the softest, most elegant necklace you've ever seen. And it's 18-karat gold. Do you know how hard it is to find a necklace in 18-karat gold? This is what you'd find at the Buckingham Palace or the Riviera, not your local jewelry store.
>
> "Ohhhh, it's so silky, so light, so delicate. They call this a herringbone necklace. Imagine the hours of work that went into creating these intricate patterns.
>
> "Perhaps you've dreamed of owning an heirloom-quality necklace like this. Today I'm going to make that dream come true by offering you a sensational buy. A necklace like this would sell for over $800 in a jewelry store. It's 13 grams of solid, 18-karat gold. I'm going to give it away to you for just $289. What a steal!"

As Bob listened, he thought to himself that the necklace would make an ideal anniversary present for his wife, Irene, so he ordered it right away. The necklace arrived about one month before their anniversary.

When Irene opened the necklace on their anniversary night, her eyes brightened. She loved it. About a week later, Irene noticed that some kinks had formed in the necklace. She tried to straighten them out, but the necklace still looked bad. Since Bob had ordered it through the mail, he couldn't take it back to the seller and have it fixed. He couldn't get his money back either. The one-month warranty had expired.

Suppose Ruth had read a book which explained how chains were priced. This could have kept her from buying a chain that was wider than she wanted because of a phony discount.

Suppose Nancy had read a book which discussed the importance of choosing a secure setting and which gave tips on how to select one. This could have prevented her from losing her diamond. Instead of only being interested in style, she would have also paid attention to the construction and setting of the ring.

Suppose Jean had read a book which indicated that the presence of a karat stamp and a trademark does not guarantee a piece is real gold. And suppose it also warned against buying jewelry offered at unbelievably low prices. She would have suspected the bangle bracelet was plated or defective.

Suppose Bob had read a book which explained that herringbone chains are prone to kinking, especially if they are soft, lightweight and delicate. Bob would have known that the advertised chain was not very durable.

To make an intelligent choice of jewelry, you should know how to evaluate it. Jewelry brochures don't tell you how to analyze the workmanship of a piece, and if they did, they wouldn't have enough space to go into much depth. Until now, there have been no books that give consumers detailed guidelines on how to choose long-wearing mountings, settings, and chains. *The Gold Jewelry Buying Guide* was written to fill this void.

When buying gold jewelry, professional assistance is also important. A knowledge of jewelry and gems will make it easier for you to select a good jeweler. You will learn far more about jewelers by examining their merchandise and discussing it with them than by asking questions such as "How long have you been in business?" "Where were you trained?" "What trade organizations do you belong to?" The answers can be fabricated, and they aren't a true indication of the jeweler's knowledge, skill, or ethics. Therefore, it's important for you yourself to be informed about jewelry. A book on judging jewelry quality not only helps you select gold jewelry, it also helps you find a good jeweler.

## What This Book Is Not

♦ It's not a guide to making a fortune on gold or gold jewelry. In fact, it recommends against buying gold jewelry for investment purposes. However, understanding the value concepts discussed in this book can increase your chances of finding good buys on gold jewelry.

♦ It's not a catalog of jewelry styles. Those can be obtained at jewelry stores.

♦ It's not a guide to making, repairing, or designing jewelry. Many helpful books have been written on these subjects; some are listed in the bibliography.

♦ It's not a price guide. Gold prices can change daily, and jewelry prices are determined by a variety of factors--quality of the craftsmanship, complexity of the design, the mode of manufacture, the geographic area where the jewelry is produced. However, a knowledge of the principles discussed in this book will help you compare prices more accurately.

♦ It's not a substitute for practical experience. To learn how to test gold and evaluate jewelry, you have to practice doing it. This book makes the learning process easier and faster.

## What This Book Is

♦ A guide to evaluating some common and important aspects of jewelry craftsmanship.

♦ An aid to avoiding fraud, with tips on detecting imitation and underkarated gold.

♦ A handy reference on gold and jewelry for laypeople and professionals.

♦ An overview of gold coins and their use in jewelry.

♦ A collection of practical tips on choosing and caring for gold jewelry.

♦ A challenge to view jewelry in terms of its craftsmanship and artistic merit rather than just its price tag.

## How to Use This Book

*The Gold Jewelry Buying Guide* is not meant to be read like a science fiction thriller or a murder mystery. If you're a layperson, you may find this book overwhelming at first. It might be advisable for you to start by looking at the pictures and by reading Chapter 2 (What's So Special About a Piece of Yellow Metal?), Chapter 14 (Finding a Good Buy), and the Table of Contents. Then you should learn the basic terminology in Chapter 3 and continue slowly, perhaps a chapter at a time.

Skip over any sections that don't interest you or that are too difficult. This book has far more information than the average person will care to learn. That's because it's also designed to be a reference. When questions arise about gold jewelry, you can avoid lengthy research by having the answers right at your fingertips.

To get the most out of *The Gold Jewelry Buying Guide*, you should try to actively use what you learn. Start examining whatever jewelry you might have at home both with and without magnification. This will help you learn to detect quality differences and distinguish between imitation and genuine gold. Take the quizzes that you'll find at the end of many of the chapters. Look around in jewelry stores and ask the professionals there to show you the difference between well-made and poorly-made jewelry.

Shopping for gold jewelry should not be a chore. It should be fun. There is no fun, though, in worrying about being deceived or in buying jewelry that doesn't last. Use this book to gain the knowledge, confidence, and independence needed to select the jewelry that is best for you. Buying jewelry represents a significant investment of time and money. Let *The Gold Jewelry Buying Guide* help make this investment a pleasurable and rewarding experience.

# 2

# What's So Special About
# A Piece of Yellow Metal?

**Gold $350 an ounce
Tantalum $25 an ounce***

Gold and tantalum are two metals that are well suited for jewelry making. Yet there's a distinct difference in their price and sales appeal. Comparing the qualities of each can help us discover why gold is so highly valued throughout the world.

**RARITY.** Both metals are rare, especially compared to metals such as iron and copper. Tantalum, however, is more rare than gold. In fact, it's so rare that many people have never heard of it. Gold has the advantage of being abundant enough so everyone can own some, but rare enough that it's not a common household item.

**RESISTANCE TO CORROSION.** Both metals resist corrosion. Tantalum, for example, is used to construct acid-resisting chemical equipment. Artifacts of gold have been preserved for centuries, demonstrating its enduring qualities.

**DENSITY & WEIGHT.** Both metals are very dense compared to other metals such as copper and silver. The specific gravity of gold is 19.32 and of tantalum, 16.60. When used in jewelry, gold is normally alloyed with other metals, thus bringing its specific gravity and weight below that of tantalum. In jewelry form, both metals have a good solid, heavy feel.

* Tantalum prices vary depending on the form and quantity in which it is sold.

**COLOR**. Normally tantalum has a dark silvery appearance, whereas pure gold is yellow. In ancient times, yellow was the most highly valued color because it represented the sun, the giver of life. Silvery white, a subordinate color, was a symbol of the moon, whose light came from the sum.

Today the choice between white or yellow tends to be a matter of personal preference. Metal value is not normally determined by color. Platinum is white (it's actually gray, but many people refer to it as a white metal), yet it's usually more expensive than gold. Silver is also white, but it costs much less.

An unusual characteristic of tantalum is that when heated above 570°F (299°C), it can turn vivid colors ranging from pink, purple, blue, turquoise, to yellow. The colors are permanent and are the result of oxidation on the surface of the metal. These colors can also be produced by an electro-chemical process called anodizing.

**MALLEABILITY**. Both tantalum and gold are very malleable, but gold is the most malleable of all metals. This means it can be rolled and hammered thinner. In fact, a couple of gold coins could be flattened out so thin that the resulting layer would cover the roof of your house. Ancient civilizations took advantage of this gold property to adorn their palaces and temples. If you visit the temples of Bangkok, you may even get a free souvenir of the gold leaf that's peeled off of roofs or walls. It's often lying on the ground, waiting to be swept away.

**DUCTILITY**. Tantalum and gold are both very ductile. This means they can be elongated or drawn into fine wire without breaking. In turn, jewelers can work these metals easily. Gold is the most ductile of all metals. The superior ductility and malleability of gold has one drawback. Gold is softer and therefore scratches and wears down more easily. To resolve this problem, gold is normally alloyed with other metals when used in jewelry. The resulting gold alloys are harder but less malleable and ductile than pure gold.

**MELTING TEMPERATURE**. Tantalum has a melting point of 5425°F (2996°C). Pure gold has a melting point of 1949°F (1065°C). The difference is significant. Special equipment is required to weld tantalum, and air has to be excluded to prevent oxidation. Joining gold is much easier.

**INDUSTRIAL POTENTIAL**. Tantalum and gold are both very important to the electronics and aerospace industries. Construction companies use glass tinted with gold for modern skyscrapers to keep them cool in summer, by reflecting the sun. Dentists couldn't get along without gold. Surgeons use tantalum for suture wire and implants because it does not react with body acids and it's not toxic to body tissues. There are many other uses as well for both metals. Industrial demand plays a large role in determining the price and availability of these and other metals.

**PUBLICITY**. We hear about gold in newspapers, on television, in economics and history courses, and from friends or relatives. Then when we go shopping, we see jewelry stores filled with gold items. This creates a desire to own gold.

Seldom, if ever, do we hear about tantalum. And relatively few people have ever seen it. The result is that there hasn't been much success selling it in the form of jewelry, despite its attractive, unique colors. One supplier of tantalum to the jewelry trade says they now only stock it in foil form. They didn't sell enough of it in wire and sheet form to make it worth their while.

Here we have two metals, tantalum and gold, so similar in so many ways. Yet gold is considered far more valuable than tantalum, even though it's not as rare. To discover why gold is so special we must look beyond its physical characteristics. It's when we examine the history of gold that we discover why it enjoys so much prestige.

Tantalum has little historical significance. It was discovered relatively recently, in 1802, by the Swedish chemist, Anders G. Ekeberg.

Gold, on the other hand, may have been known to man since his beginning. In the Bible, it is both the first metal and first atomic element to be mentioned. Adam and Eve didn't have far to go to find gold.

> And a river went out of Eden to water the garden; and from thence it was parted, and became into four heads. The name of the first is Pisin: that is it which compasseth the whole land of Havilah, where there is gold; And the gold of that land is good:
> Genesis 2:10-12.

Primitive man was able to find gold in its free form in riverbeds when obtaining water. As a nugget, gold could be an attractive jewelry item. Man soon linked gold to the sun god, who provided him with light, warmth, and crops. Consequently, gold became important for the religious objects and ceremonies of early civilizations.

Around 700 BC, gold became a basis for economic life. Gyges of Lydia (what is now south-central Turkey) established the first mint to put the seal of his kingdom on uniform lumps of gold. (These gold lumps were an alloy of about 75% gold and 25% silver called "electrum.")

About 550 BC, the Lydian king, Croesus, became the first to introduce coins of pure gold. His royal stamp on the coin was a guarantee as to their weight and purity. Since then, gold coins have been minted by almost every government. The circulation of these coins with the seal of the government served as an ideal advertisement for gold. "Gold" and "high value" became synonymous.

It was primarily the lure of gold that brought so many Spaniards to Mexico and South America during the 16th century. Three hundred years later, in 1849, one of the greatest gold rushes of all time drew more than 40,000 diggers to California. The population of Australia grew from around 400,000 in 1851 to 1,200,000 in just ten years largely as the result of the discovery of gold. In 1896, more than 60,000 men flocked to the Yukon in Canada near Alaska. Gold panning continues there still. Gold in Brazil, British Columbia, South Dakota, Nevada, North Carolina, Georgia, and New Zealand have also created mass movements of population.

The largest gold find ever was in 1886 at the Witwatersrand Reef in South Africa. Since then, South Africa has become the world's largest producer of gold (about 30%), followed by the USSR, the US, Australia and Canada.

The gold rushes of the 19th century had a phenomenal impact. They stimulated shipping, commerce, and manufacturing throughout the world. The huge increase in the supply of gold inflated the world's currencies and led to the adoption of the gold standard by most of the leading nations (although later it was abandoned). The transportation system of the United States was significantly expanded in order to deliver supplies to miners throughout the West. Australia and the western part of North America became important commercial centers. A large percentage of the people in these areas would not be there today had it not been for the quest for gold.

On a worldwide and historical basis, gold has always remained the king of money. It's accepted everywhere as a medium of exchange. This, combined with its portability, has made it the most important investment for people living under oppressive or unstable governments. Thanks to gold, many Vietnamese refugees were able to start a new life in other countries. People in Taiwan are buying gold in unusually large quantities now. It gives them a sense of security. Someday they may need it as a "plane ticket" to a safe haven.

The natural beauty of gold, along with its workability, high value, and history has made it the world's most important jewelry metal. Even though in Japan, brides prefer platinum wedding rings, in most other cultures, a gold band is the traditional choice.

A gold jewelry piece is even more than an object of beauty or a commitment of love. It's an asset of enduring value, which can be passed on from one generation to another. It is also a reminder of an extraordinary metal, one which has changed the destiny of mankind.

# 3

# Gold Terms & Notation

**O**ld gold. To the non-jeweler, this term might signify "gold mined in ancient times." To a jeweler, it usually refers to scrap gold with solder and impurities, which make it porous and weak. Freshly refined gold would be called **new gold**.

This book uses many terms that may be new to the layperson. The purpose of this chapter is to make your reading easier by defining basic terms related to gold jewelry.

## Terms Related to Gold Content

| | |
|---|---|
| **Fine gold** | Gold containing no other elements or metals. It's also called pure gold or 24K (24 karat) gold and has a fineness of 999. |
| **Fineness** | The amount of gold in relation to 1000 parts. For example, gold with a fineness of 750 has 750 parts (75%) gold and 250 parts of other metals. |
| **Gold alloy** | A mixture of gold with other metal(s) formed by melting them together. Gold is alloyed (combined) with metals such as silver, copper, zinc, and nickel to reduce its cost and change characteristics such as its color and hardness. |
| **Karat (Carat)** | A measure of gold purity. One karat is 1/24 pure, so 24 karat is pure gold. Do not confuse "karat," the unit of gold purity, with "carat," the unit of weight for gemstones. These two words originate from the same source, the Italian "carato" and the Greek "karation" which mean "fruit of the carob tree." In ancient times, carob beans were used as counterweights when weighing gems and gold. |

Outside the US, "karat" is often spelled "carat," particularly in countries which are members of the British Commonwealth.

**Karat gold**     A gold alloy, which in the United States must have a fineness of at least 10K. In Britain and Canada, it must be at least 9K. There's a possibility that 10K will become the legal gold standard in Britain and Canada too.

**Plumb gold (KP)**     In general usage, it means gold that has the same purity as the mark stamped on it. Therefore, 14KP means gold that is really 14K. Prior to 1978 in the US, 13K gold jewelry which had been soldered could be stamped 14K. According to current US and Canadian law, the pure gold content must be within 3 parts per thousand of the stamped karat mark for unsoldered items and 7 parts per thousand for soldered items. This means that technically all marked gold sold now is plumb gold. In reality, not all gold jewelry is. When jewelers describe their jewelry as plumb gold, they are emphasizing that they abide by the law.

In the US and Canada, gold solders do not have to comply with the plumb-gold laws. A 14K solder might range from 12 to 14K. If jewelers want to specify that they want a solder which is actually 14K, they may request a plumb-gold solder.

**Pure gold**     Same as fine gold

**Solid gold**     Gold that is not hollow. Even though legally in the US, "solid gold" can only be used for 24K gold, it more commonly refers to karat gold which is not hollow or layered.

# Weights, Measures and Marks

**Avoirdupois weight**     The weight system used in the US for food and people and almost everything except precious metals and gems. One pound avoirdupois equals 16 ounces.

**Grain**     A measurement of weight equaling 1/24 of a pennyweight. This was one of the earliest units of weight for gold. It was originally the equivalent of one grain of wheat.

**Gram**     The most widespread unit of weight for gold jewelry. See Table 3.1 for equivalent weights.

**Hallmark**

An official mark stamped on gold, silver or platinum objects to indicate their quality, origin, and maker. The term refers to the Goldsmith's Hall in London, which has overseen the marking of gold in England since 1300. Hallmarking systems are found in European countries such as Belgium, France, Britain, Germany, Holland, Italy, Portugal, and Denmark. Figure 3.1 is an example of a British hallmark.

**Fig. 3.1** A British hallmark. From left to right is the maker's mark, the British-made standard mark, the purity numbers, the assay office mark, and the year letter. *Diagram courtesy Gemological Institute of America.*

**Pennyweight**

Unit of weight equaling 1/20 of a troy ounce. In the Middle Ages it was the weight of a silver penny in Britain. Now pennyweight is used mainly in the American jewelry trade.

**Quality mark**

A set of numbers, letters, or symbols stamped on metal to indicate its type and content (fig 3.2). For example 18K means 75% gold, 900 Plat. means 90% platinum. In the US, jewelry which does not cross state lines has not been required to have a quality mark.

**Fig. 3.2** A quality mark with the trademark below.

**Fig. 3.3** A hand engraving. *Photo courtesy of the engraver, Hans Kober*

| | |
|---|---|
| **Tael** | Chinese gold weight. 1 tael = 1.2034 ounces troy of .999 fineness. |
| **Trademark** | A mark that indicates the manufacturer, importer or seller of an item (whoever stands behind its quality mark). In the US, trademarks must be registered with the Patent and Trademark Office, and trademarked items must have a quality mark. Also, any item that bears a quality mark is supposed to have a US registered trademark. There is little enforcement of this law, though. Consequently, a lot of jewelry marked 10, 14 or 18K is not trademarked (fig 3.2). |
| **Troy ounce** | The standard unit of weight for gold. It may have been named after a weight used at the annual fair at Troyes in France during the Middle Ages. |
| **Troy weight** | The system of weights used in the US and England for gold and silver, in which 1 pound equals 12 ounces, and 1 ounce equals 20 pennyweights. It should not be confused with avoirdupois weight. |

Table 3.1

| Weight Conversion Table | |
|---|---|
| 1 pennyweight (dwt) | = 1.555 g  = 0.05 oz t  = 0.055 oz av  = 7.776 cts |
| 1 troy ounce (oz t) | = 31.103 g  = 1.097 oz av  = 20 dwt  = 155.51 cts |
| 1 ounce avoirdupois (oz av) | = 28.3495 g  = 0.911 oz t  = 18.229 dwt  = 141.75 cts |
| 1 carat (ct) | = 0.2 g  = 0.006 oz t  = 0.007 oz av  = 0.31 dwt |
| 1 gram (g) | = 5 cts  = 0.032 oz t  = 0.035 oz av  = 0.643 dwt |

# Terms Related to Imitation Gold

| | |
|---|---|
| **Base metal** | A nonprecious metal such as brass or copper |
| **Electroplating** | A quick and inexpensive way to make base metal look like gold. The metal object is dipped in a gold plating solution and then an electrical |

current is used to coat the object with a thin layer of gold. The thickness of the gold depends upon the amount and duration of the current. For an item to be called **gold electroplate** (commonly stamped **GEP**) in the US, the gold layer must be at least 7/1,000,000 of an inch thick. If the layer is thinner, then the item is described as **gold flashed** or **gold washed**.

| | |
|---|---|
| **Gold filled (GF)** | Composed of a layer of gold mechanically bonded to a base metal using heat and pressure. In the US, the layer must be at least 10K gold and 1/20th of the total weight of the object. |
| **Gold overlay** | Same as gold filled except the gold layer is thinner. It can be from 1/20th to 1/40th of the total weight of the object. |
| **Gold plate (GP)** **Rolled gold plate (RGP)** | Same as gold overlay. An example of how it might be indicated on indicated on a jewelry piece is **"1/40 12 Kt RGP,"** meaning that the piece has been mechanically bonded with a layer of 12K gold which is 1/40th of the total weight of the piece. Canadian law does not allow plated items to be stamped. |
| **Vermeil** | Sterling silver covered with at least 120/millionths of an inch of fine gold. The layer of gold may be either electroplated or mechanically bonded. |

# Decorative Techniques and Finishes

| | |
|---|---|
| **Bark finish** | A surface texture resembling tree bark (color photo 3a). |
| **Bright polish** | Mirror-like finish. It may also be called a **high polish**. |
| **Brushed finish** | Tiny parallel lines are scratched on the surface with a wire brush creating soft, diffused reflections. |
| **Chasing** | A technique of indenting and raising a relief design into metal from the front using chisels and punches. |
| **Embossing** | A technique of creating a raised design by pushing metal out from its reverse side with hammers and punches. The process can also be done mechanically using dies. |

**Enameling**    Fusion of a colored glassy substance to metal to create a design.

**Engraving**    A line design cut into metal. Most engraving today is done by machine, but skilled hand engravers are still in demand. Figure 3.3 is an example of a hand engraving.

**Etching**    A process of using acids to create a design on metal by corrosion.

**Filigree**    A delicate, openwork design often made by bending and soldering fine wires.

**Florentine finish**    Cross-hatched pattern with coarser lines than a brushed finish (fig. 3.4).

**Fusion**    Melting metal to produce interesting forms and textures. Also, the process of uniting two metals using heat and no solder.

**Glassbeaded finish**    A matte finish achieved by blasting metal with minute glass beads using a sandblasting machine. Part of the surface of the pendant on the book cover has a glassbeaded finish. Fingerprints on this glass-beaded surface won't show. If it had been blasted with sand, the finish would be coarser and would tend to darken from the skin oil. Some jewelers resolve this problem with sandblasted finishes by touching the whole sandblasted area with their fingers to give it a uniform color.

**Granulation**    Tiny metal balls fused to a metal base. No solder is used.

**Milgraining**    A beaded line pattern made by hand or machine (fig. 3.5). It's often used as an ornamental border on the edges of wedding bands.

**Fig. 3.4** A florentine finish magnified 10X.

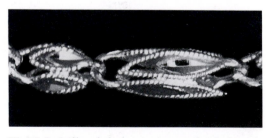

**Fig. 3.5** Milgraining on a marquis chain.

| | |
|---|---|
| **Matte finish** | A dull, non-reflective finish. |
| **Oxidizing** | A process of darkening or coloring a metal surface through oxidation. For example, a flame with oxygen can produce a dark antique-like surface finish on karat gold. The lower the fineness of the gold, the darker the result can be. |
| **Repoussé** | The process of raising a design in sheet metal by punching up the reverse side. Repoussé is then finished from the front by chasing. |
| **Roll printing** | A technique of transferring a texture from one material to another. A "sandwich" made of a sheet of metal and a texturing material is passed through a rolling mill under great pressure. The metal is embossed with the reverse image of the material. |
| **Sandblasted finish** | A matte finish made by blasting metal with sand (color photo 3b). It is grainier than a glassbeaded finish. Some people in the trade may use the term "sandblasted" to also mean "glassbeaded" since both finishes are produced by a sandblasting machine. |
| **Satin finish** | A very finely brushed surface texture resembling satin. |

Terminology becomes more meaningful when we see how it is applied to actual examples. Figures 3.6 and 3.7 illustrate how some of the techniques and finishes listed above can be combined to create interesting pieces.

A fiberglass-brushed finish has been used on the disk portion of the 18K gold pin/pendant shown in figure 3.6. As an accent, abstract lines were engraved. An attractive contrast is provided by the high polish of the zigzag design. This zigzag pattern is detachable and was added so the piece could also be worn as a pin.

**Fig. 3.6** A pin/pendant with a fiberglass-brushed finish. *Photo copyright Levine Design.*

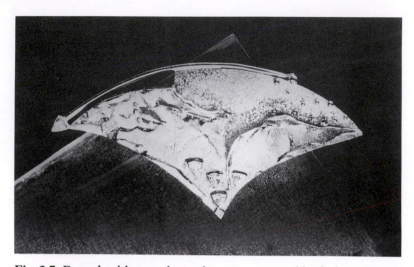

**Fig. 3.7** Brooch with granules and textures created by fusion, chasing and roll printing. Photo courtesy of the designer and craftsman, Richard Kimball.

The hand-fabricated brooch in figure 3.7 (color photo 3b) is part of a series of pieces called "pocket maps." Its layout is based on Chinese landscape paintings of the 15th and 16th centuries. The piece was designed to be read topographically as from an airplane or horizontally from bottom to top (near to far) like a painting. The 18K-gold land formations were created by fusion and chasing. The white palladium portion, representing either water or sky, was textured by roll printing. Granulation was added as a visual accent.

# Miscellaneous Terms

**Brass**     An alloy of copper and zinc that is often used in costume jewelry. Copper is the main component.

**Bronze**    An alloy composed mainly of copper and tin. Zinc or other elements may be present. Copper is the principal component.

**Findings**    Metal components used for jewelry construction or repair such as clasps, settings, studs, and safety chains.

**Mounting**   The metal part of a jewelry piece before the stones are set into it.

**Refining**     The process of removing impurities from a precious metal.

**Shank**        The part of a ring that encircles the finger and is attached to the stone setting(s).

**Solder**       A metal or metallic alloy used to join metals. Solder is designed to melt at a lower temperature than the metal to be joined. The terms **easy, medium**, and **hard solders** are used to describe solders with progressively higher melting points. Normally, hard solder is first used on a piece since it melts at the highest temperature. Medium and then easy solders are used afterwards. This technique permits the jeweler to solder a piece together without melting previously made joints.

**Soldering**   The process of fusing two pieces of metal together with solder.

# Natural Nugget Gold Jewelry

Jewelry with pieces of **placer gold** (gold found mainly in river and stream beds) is referred to as **nugget gold jewelry** or **natural nugget jewelry**. Most of this jewelry is produced in Western North AMerica. Nugget gold jewelry had its first serious commercial start in Canada with the Klondike Gold Rush of the late 1890's. Many elaborate nugget items were made for the wealthy, for example, 60" graduated nugget chains. Pins and buckles inlaid with natural nuggets were popular with tourists. Nugget gold wedding bands became a traditional item for residents of the areas connected with placer gold mining. The watch and ring in color photo 3d are examples of nugget jewelry currently made in the Klondike Region. The nuggets in this photo were recovered from the Dawson City area of the Yukon, Canada between the years 1973 and 1992. Jewelry and nuggets from British Columbia are shown in figure 3.8.

Gold nuggets are not comprised of entirely *pure* gold. The highest assays average about 96%. The overall average ranges from 80 to 85% pure gold. The purity can vary greatly within individual gold claims. In the Klondike gold district the average purity ranges from about 60% to 76%, yet their are several creeks in this district that average 85%-90% pure gold.

Natural gold nuggets are not necessarily a uniform yellow color. They can also have a subtle white, green, pink, red, or orange tone depending on the other metals naturally alloyed with them. In a few limited areas, platinum nuggets are also recovered with the gold. Platinum nuggets very rarely exceed more than one gram in weight. Gold nuggets, on the other hand, range from flour or dust size particles to nuggets weighing as much as 2,000 ounces.

For jewelry purposes, nuggets are measured according to screen sizes. The smallest size used is **#16 mesh** (16 openings per inch). The largest size is **#4 mesh** (4 openings per inch).

Genuine nugget jewelry should not be confused with imitation-nugget (nugget-look) jewelry, which sells for much less. Compare the imitation nugget ring in figure 3.9 to the nugget jewelry in fig. 3.8 and color photo 3d. The imitation ring was entirely cast from molten metal. The genuine jewelry has natural nuggets which are individually soldered to the piece.

**Fig. 3.8** A pair of 18K earrings inlaid with #12 mesh-screen size gold nuggets from the Central Yukon territory. Their fine gold content is 850. Center background, 18K ring inlaid with #8 and #10 mesh gold nuggets and #14 natural platinum nuggets. Right background 18K ring inlaid with #8 mesh size nugget gold. The gold nuggets in the rings have a fineness of 900 and are from the Cariboo district of British Columbia. Center foreground, 18K ring inlaid with natural platinum nuggets from southern British Columbia. *Photo courtesy Canadian Placer Gold Sales Ltd.*

Some differences between man-made and natural nuggets are as follows:

♦ Man-made nuggets have a higher density than natural ones. As a consequence, when manufactured nuggets are dropped on a hard surface, they tend to produce a high-pitched ringing sound, whereas natural nuggets have a duller sound.

**Fig.3.9** Imitation-nugget ring

♦ Man-made nuggets have a harder feel than natural placer nuggets.

♦ Man-made nuggets are more uniform in color than natural ones. This is either because they have been cast from the same metal or because they have been plated. Be suspicious if the color of the nuggets matches the color of the karat gold mounting exactly.

Some of the factors that affect the price and quality of natural gold nugget jewelry are listed below:

♦ The shape of the nuggets. The more unusual the shape, the higher the price. When natural materials such as quartz are present, leave them intact because they add interest and therefore value to the piece.

♦ The size of the nuggets. The larger the nugget the higher the price per gram or per ounce. Some of the larger nuggets sell at premiums of three or four times their gold value.

♦ The color of the nuggets. Deep, rich natural colors command higher prices than pale colors.

♦ Careful soldering of the nuggets to the mountings. No gold solder should be visible. Better crafted pieces require more time and skill, and as a consequence, tend to cost more.

♦ Careful placement of the nuggets on the mountings. Nuggets that are #16 mesh size and larger should be placed so that are individually visible on the jewelry piece.

(Most of the information for this section on nugget jewelry is from an informational letter by Canadian Placer Gold Sales Limited, Vancouver, British, Columbia.)

# Quiz   (Chapters 1, 2, & 3)

## True or False?

1.   A trademark is a hallmark.

2.   If a piece is stamped 18KP, then this means it is plated with 18K gold.

3.   One ounce of gold is heavier than one ounce of perfume.

4.   12K gold contains 50% fine gold.

5.   The carat can be either a measure of gold purity or gemstone weight.

6.   One ounce of fine gold would normally be worth more than a one ounce natural gold nugget since nuggets are not pure gold.

7.   "Gold overlay," "gold plate," and "rolled gold plate" are equivalent terms.

8.   If a salesperson has a gemologist diploma, this means he or she knows a lot about jewelry craftsmanship.

9.   A pennyweight of gold is heavier than a gram.

10.   Natural gold nuggets are not as dense and evenly colored as man-made nuggets.

11.   The main reason gold is so valuable is that it is very rare.

12.   In the United States and Canada, any jewelry described as real gold must be at least 10 karats.

13.   Vermeil is sterling silver covered with at least 120 millionths of an inch of gold.

14.   The terms "satin," "florentine," "brushed," and "bark" all refer to decorative jewelry finishes.

15.   If a jewelry piece has a trademark next to the karat or fineness stamp, then it is real gold with the same gold content as the stamp indicates.

# Answers

1. F   A trademark is the mark of the manufacturer, seller, or importer that stands behind the quality mark. A hallmark is a series of symbols that include both the quality and manufacturer's mark as well as other symbols. The United States does not have a hallmarking system.

2. F   18KP stands for 18K plumb gold, not plated gold.

3. T   Gold is measured in ounces troy and perfume in ounces avoirdupois. The troy ounce is heavier than the avoirdupois ounce.

4. T   12K gold is 12/24ths pure gold or in other words 50% gold.

5. T   In countries of the British Commonwealth, "carat" has a dual meaning. However, in the US a distinction is made between "karat" the measure of gold purity and "carat" the unit of gemstone weight.

6. F   Large gold nuggets sell at high premiums and therefore are worth a lot more than their pure gold value

7. T

8. F   A gemologist diploma is awarded to those who have completed studies on gem identification, diamonds and colored stones and passed the required tests. It gives no indication of their ability to judge jewelry craftsmanship. There are people who have no diplomas and who know a great deal about gems and jewelry craftsmanship. It's better to judge people by what they know than by the diplomas they hold.

9. T

10. T

11. F   There are metals that are more rare than gold which sell for a lot less.

12. F   In Canada, the legal standard is 9K, not 10K as it is in the US.

13. T

14. T

15. F   Professional gold buyers know that trademarks can be faked. Laypeople should also be aware of this. Even if an unscrupulous jeweler stamps his true initials or trademark next to an inaccurate karat mark, he doesn't have much to fear. It's unlikely that a 12K piece stamped 14K, for example, will ever be checked with an assay test in the US.

# 4

# Manufacturing Methods

Suppose you're looking at two 14K solitaire rings. One was made from components punched out of solid gold by a machine, and the other was formed by casting molten gold into a mold. Which ring would probably wear better? Which ring would cost more to make?

The gold of the machine-made ring would normally be harder and denser. Therefore, it would wear better. The manufacturing cost of each ring would depend largely on the number produced. In smaller quantities, casting is definitely cheaper.

It will be easier to understand the chapters on quality analysis in this book, if you know how jewelry is produced. This chapter presents the four basic methods of making jewelry--casting, stamping (die-striking), electroforming, and hand fabrication. In addition, it explains how combining these methods may be advantageous when producing a piece.

## Lost Wax Casting

Lost wax casting dates back at least to 1500 BC, when the Egyptians were using it. For awhile, this method disappeared, but in recent years, it has become the most widely used manufacturing process. Lost wax casting involves a series of steps. They are as follows:

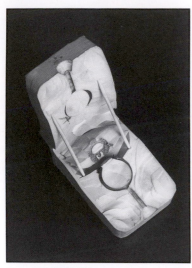

**Fig. 4.1**  Rubber mold

**Fig. 4.2**  Wax model

1.  **A model (jewelry piece) is made in metal** from an original design.  Sometimes the model is a piece which has already been cast.  (Often the first step in lost wax casting is to carve a model in wax.  The rubber molding process, described in steps 1 to 3, is relatively new compared to the modeling of wax by hand carving.)

2.  **A rubber mold of the metal model is made** (fig. 4.1).  The model is placed in a rectangular frame, rubber is packed around it, the rubber is heated so it flows around the model and is vulcanized into a solid block.

3.  **A wax copy(s) of the model is made** by injecting wax into the mold through a hole (fig. 4.2).  An original wax model may be carved or sculpted instead (color photo 4b).  It's usually faster to carve a wax model than to make a metal model.

4.  **The wax model(s) are attached to a base** either in the form of a tree or a donut (fig 4.3).  The tree may be formed with several wax models all made from the same mold or with different-style models.

5.  **The wax tree or donut is covered with a material like plaster of paris**, called investment.  This is allowed to harden.

6.  **The plaster mold is heated.**  The wax melts and pours out of a hole in the base.  A hollow plaster mold is left.

7. **Molten gold is thrust into the plaster mold** by centrifugal force or vacuum. The open spaces left by the melted wax are filled with the gold. The metal is allowed to solidify.

8. **The hot plaster mold is plunged into water.** The sudden change of temperature makes the plaster shatter, leaving gold copies of the wax models (fig. 4.3). These are cleaned and polished.

It's best for a cast piece to be made from an original model. Detail is lost whenever a piece is recopied. Also, each time a rubber mold is made, the resulting wax and copy are a little smaller and thinner than the original.

**Fig. 4.3** "Tree" with wax models and the resulting gold castings. *Photo courtesy Stamper Black Hills Gold Jewelry.*

Casting offers the following benefits:

## Advantages of casting

♦ It's a relatively quick way of making several identical pieces.

♦ It offers unlimited design possibilities (color photo 4a). You can even draw your own designs and have the jeweler transfer them to a wax model. Figure 4.4 shows pieces that were custom designed for people with special interests.

♦ It's economical when many pieces are produced from the same mold. One-of-a-kind cast pieces, however, can be just as costly as those which are hand-fabricated.

♦ It's an easy way to make copies or matching pieces. For example, a necklace might be used to make a mold for a matching bracelet. A lost earring can possibly be replaced by copying the remaining earring, providing it is not too thin.

## Disadvantages of casting

♦ Due to their lower density, cast pieces don't wear as well as those which are stamped and hand-fabricated.

♦ Cast gold is less suitable for fine engraving because it's more porous.

♦ Casting usually requires more cleanup and finishing than other methods. As a result, cast jewelry is often rougher and duller underneath, especially in hard to reach areas.

**Figure 4.4** Dog-paw bracelet and earrings for a dog trainer, turkey-head tie-tac for a turkey hunter, and two styles of leaf earrings. All were hand carved in wax and then cast with 14K yellow gold. *Photo courtesy of Erik Jewelers.*

## Stamping (Die-Striking)

Another ancient technique for making jewelry is **stamping**, which in the United States, is also called **die-striking**. In this process, metal is punched between two carved metal blocks called **dies**, creating a form and design. The metal becomes very dense and strong as the hydraulic presses squeeze it between the dies at pressures of up to 25 tons per square inch.

The quality of stamped jewelry has greatly improved over the years. In some cases, it even looks like it's hand fabricated. The stamping process is often used to make earrings, pendants, coins, ring shanks, settings (fig. 4.5), and fancy Italian chains such as the San Marco and hugs & kisses shown in Chapter 7. Its positive and negative points are as follows:

## Advantages of stamping

♦ The quality is consistent.

♦ In large quantities, it's economical.

♦ Once the dies are made, it's a faster production process than the other methods.

♦ Stamped items usually wear better than cast items, due to their high density.

♦ Stamped pieces require little cleanup before polishing.

♦ Stamped jewelry can take a very high polish because of its density.

♦ Stamped pieces can be thinner than those which are cast. Therefore they may provide a bigger look at a lower price.

♦ Stamped gold is ideal for engraving, due to its high density.

**Fig. 4.5** Die-struck shank and head (setting)

## Disadvantages of stamping

♦ It's not suitable for small-scale manufacturing because of the high cost of the dies and equipment.

♦ It's a longer process than casting if the dies are not readily available. To have dies made may take a month.

♦ Design options are limited.

# Electroforming

**Electroforming** is a technique of forming metal objects by electrically depositing the metal over a mold. The mold, which may be made of a material such as wax, epoxy resin, or silicone rubber, is later removed, leaving a metal shell.

The process of electroforming originated in the 1830's with the birth of electroplating (Rod Edwards, *The Technique of Jewelry*, p.202). It became a convenient and extremely accurate

**Fig. 4.6** Electroformed earrings. Photo courtesy *Maurice Badler Fine Jewelry.*

way for museums to reproduce antique pieces. Originally, gold electroforming required a very high karat gold--at least 23.5K. But in the early 1980's, a French jewelry manufacturer developed a way of making electroformed pieces out of 14 and 18K gold. Since then, electroformed jewelry has become increasingly popular.

The advantages and drawbacks of electroformed jewelry are listed below:

## Advantages of electroformed jewelry:

♦ It provides a big look at a relatively low price.

♦ It's lightweight and therefore ideal for earrings (fig. 4.6).

♦ It can show minute detail like one would see in a fine engraving.

## Disadvantages of electroformed jewelry:

♦ It dents very easily. The average thickness of the higher quality pieces is about .007 of an inch, so special care is required. Electroforming would be an unsuitable process for making bracelets or rings.

♦ It cannot be repaired. Some manufacturers, however, offer a lifetime replacement warranty.

♦ It usually costs more per gram than stamped and cast jewelry. This is because expensive equipment is used to make it, and it tends to be produced in lower quantities.

♦ Even though gems have been set in electroformed jewelry, the thinness of the metal often makes setting impossible.

♦ It's usually difficult to add a textured finish to electroformed jewelry due to the thinness of the metal.

Electroformed jewelry can vary in quality depending on the manufacturer. Some pieces may have a metal thickness of only .003 of an inch. Others may lack the bright polish or stronger post assembly of a better quality piece. The thinner more fragile pieces may be cheaper; but if they don't last as long, they shouldn't be considered a better buy.

# Hand Fabrication

Hand fabrication is the oldest way of making jewelry. It involves the use of hand tools. The piece is entirely made with hand procedures such as hammering, sawing, soldering, filing, carving, setting, finishing. Often the pieces are one-of-a-kind; but several pieces may be produced from the same design, thereby decreasing the time and cost of fabrication.

In Europe, a higher percentage of the jewelry is hand-fabricated compared to the United States. Just as many Europeans enjoy buying bread from their local bakery, they also like the personal touch of dealing with a jeweler who makes a piece from start to finish. Other reasons for buying hand-fabricated jewelry are as follows:

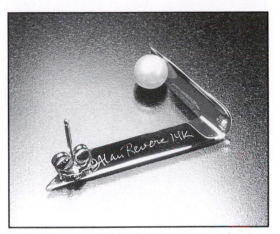

Fig. 4.7 Goldsmith's signature on the back of a hand-fabricated earring.

## Advantages of hand fabrication

♦ It requires less cleanup and finishing than casting. Therefore the backs of hand-fabricated pieces are often smoother and brighter than those which are cast.

♦ It allows exclusivity and great versatility. Each item can be unique.

♦ It shows the human quality and individuality of the craftsman.

♦ Hand-worked gold can be stronger and denser than cast gold.

♦ Hand-fabricated jewelry can be more lightweight than if it were cast. This means it's an ideal way to make comfortable earrings.

## Disadvantages of hand fabrication

♦ It's usually a very time-consuming process, Sometimes, though, hand fabrication is easier and faster than other methods.

♦ It is often more expensive, due to the extra time required.

Occasionally people neglect to consider hand-crafted jewelry because they assume it will be too costly. This is a mistake. Hand-fabricated jewelry can be affordable. An example is the earring shown in figure 4.7 and color photo 4e. The signature of the goldsmith who designed and made it is on the back. Hand-crafted pieces like this have an important role--they offer buyers the privilege of owning a product of the creative mind rather than of a machine.

## Handmade Jewelry

Within the jewelry industry, the term "handmade" has a variety of meanings and connotations. According to the Federal Trade Commission of the United States, the term "handmade" should only be applied to jewelry which is made entirely by hand methods and tools. If any part of the piece is cast or die-struck, it is not handmade. Appraisers often use this meaning for the term "handmade."

Some jewelers describe custom-made jewelry as handmade if most of the work is done by hand. They reason that a cast piece made from a hand-carved wax and then finished and set by hand can require just as much creativity and work as a hand-fabricated piece.

Chain manufacturers make a distinction between chain which is handmade and machine-made. If a rope chain, for example, is assembled by hand, it is considered handmade even if the loops have been formed by a machine.

Since "handmade" is a more generic, less precise term than "hand-fabricated," goldsmiths generally prefer to have their hand-crafted pieces described as "hand-fabricated." This way it's clear that no part of the piece is cast or die-struck. To a few people, "handmade" may even sometimes have negative connotations such as "homespun" or "unsophisticated."

Since there are a variety of meanings for "handmade," it is best to ask salespeople and jewelers to define what they mean when they use this term. This will prevent misunderstandings from occurring.

## Why Manufacturing Methods are Often Combined

Jewelers like to take advantage of the benefits of the various manufacturing techniques. For example, the diamonds of engagement rings are often put in die-struck or hand-fabricated prong settings. Since the metal of these settings is usually harder and denser, they can hold the diamonds more securely than those which are cast. Also the shape and thickness of the prongs is generally more consistent.

In his book, *The Retail Jeweller's Guide* (p. 200), Kenneth Blakemore mentions that it is common practice in Britain to use a cast head and hand-fabricated shank to make a gem ring. "The drawn wire (hand-fabricated) shank has more elasticity than has a cast one, and will better stand up to the stretching entailed in sizing it."

**3a** A bark-like texture on a cast and hand-finished necklace with matching earrings. *Photo courtesy Maurice Badler Fine Jewelry. Photo by the Goldmark Group.*

**3b** Sandblasted finish on a replica of an ancient coin.

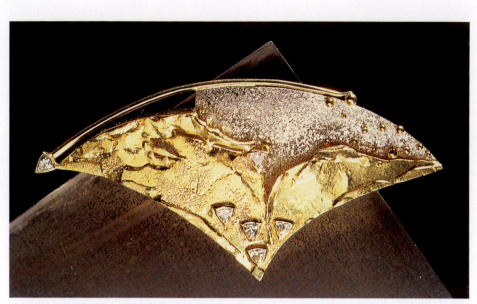

**3c** Hand-fabricated 18K gold and palladium brooch with six triangular diamonds. *Photo courtesy Richard Kimball.*

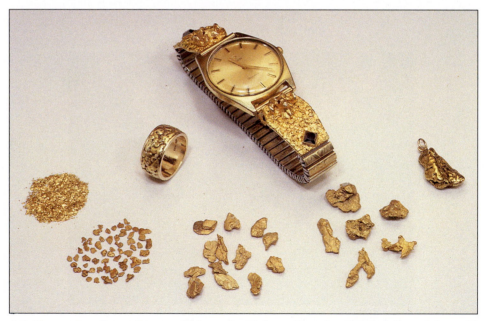

**3d** Nugget jewelry and raw gold from the Yukon, Canada. Lower left to right: gold dust, coarse gold, small nuggets, large nuggets, collector nugget.

**4a** A custom-designed silver and gold cast brooch

**4b** Wax sculpture used to make the brooch above. *Photo courtesy of the sculptor, Peggy Croft.*

**4c** Electroformed pendant. *Photo courtesy Maurice Badler Fine Jewelry. Photo by the Goldmark Group.*

**4d** A cast bezel setting, custom-designed for the 8.39 carat scapolite.

**4e** Hand-fabricated earring of 14K gold set with a cultured pearl. *Photo courtesy Alan Revere Jewelry Design.*

**4f** An 18K white-gold brooch with cast frame and hand-crafted wirework. *Photo courtesy The Roxx Limited.*

**4g** A handmade 24K chain and 22K bracelet. The loop-in-loop chain is typical of SE Asian and early Mediterranean jewelry dating back to the 4th and 5th century BC. The bracelet is a recent copy of old "Rattanakosan style." *Photo courtesy of Asian Institute of Gemological Sciences.*

**10a** Top: 14K Italian-made chain, bottom: lighter yellow 14K American-made chain.

**5a & b** Front and back of a cast 18K gold brooch custom-designed for the amethysts. Note the attractive finish. *Photos courtesy Forest Jewelers.*

**5c** Back of the brooch on the front cover--another example of a high-quality finish.

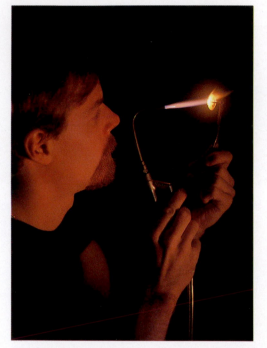

**5d** Jeweler annealing metal (heating it to make it more workable). *Photo courtesy of the jeweler, Erik Anderson.*

**6a** Unacceptable workmanship. Note the unseated sapphire, the pitted metal, the irregular and bulky prongs, and the burned surface of the sapphire which was caused by a jeweler's torch.

Long parallel lines or rims on an item can be of a more consistent thickness if they are hand-fabricated rather than cast. It's often better to make bracelet and necklace catches by hand so they can be an integral part of the piece.

Figure 4.8 (color photo 4f) is an example of how a jeweler can combine methods to produce a high quality piece in a cost-effective way. The scroll-like frame was cast from a hand-carved wax. A rubber mold of it was made so the design cost could be shared by other pieces cast from it. The wire design and setting were hand-fabricated. It was easier to bend the wire than to carve a wax and cast and finish it. In addition, the wire patterns are cleaner and more attractive. When other scroll frames are cast from the mold, the setting and wire design can be changed to give each piece a unique look.

**Fig. 4.8** Brooch with cast frame and hand-crafted wirework. *Photo courtesy The Roxx Limited.*

Sometimes people regard cast and stamped jewelry as cheap. This is wrong. High-quality jewelry can be made with any of the manufacturing methods. What counts is that the jeweler is skilled and that the method(s) chosen suit the needs of the buyer and the piece.

# Chapter 4 Quiz

## True or false?

1. Die-struck metal usually wears better than cast metal.

2. Casting would probably be the fastest and least expensive method of producing 100 wedding bands of the same style.

3. Casting would probably be the fastest and most economical way of producing 20,000 earrings with a rounded ridge design.

4. "Hand-fabricated" is just another term for "handmade."

5. The main disadvantage of electroformed jewelry is that it dents easily and can't be repaired.

6. Hand-fabricated pieces can usually have a cleaner finish and more strength than cast items.

7. Electroformed earrings are very comfortable due to their light weight.

8. The main reason for using a die-struck setting is to cut costs.

9. Sometimes, it may be faster & easier to fabricate a piece by hand than to cast and finish it.

10. Hand-fabricated pieces are always more valuable than those which are cast.

## Answers:

1. **T** Because it's denser and less porous than cast metal.
2. **T**
3. **F** Die-striking may be faster and more economical. High-quality stamped earrings could be punched out very quickly, making it cost effective to pay for dies. In addition, the earrings could probably be lighter in weight than if they were cast, thereby cutting costs on gold. Cast mountings with rounded ridges tend to be difficult and time consuming to finish properly.
4. **F** Even though these two expressions sometimes have the same meaning, "handmade" is a broader and more generic term. On occasion, it carries a negative connotation, unlike "hand-fabricated" which is always perceived as a positive term.
5. **T**
6. **T**
7. **T**
8. **F** Cast settings are just as economical, but die-struck settings are stronger and wear better.
9. **T**
10. **F** Even though hand-fabricated pieces tend to cost more, a well-made cast piece would be more valuable than a poorly-made hand-fabricated one, assuming that their style and weight is the same.

# 5

# Judging the Mounting

Can you be assured that a new car will be safe and mechanically sound just because highly trained engineers designed it? Of course not. Likewise, you can't assume that a piece of jewelry is of high quality just because it was made or sold by a well-established firm.

No matter how beautiful a car or jewelry piece is, if it requires constant repairs or is uncomfortable, it's not worth buying. Consumers can learn about cars in magazines which rate them according to their performance and repair records. Jewelry, however, tends to be a blind purchase. It shouldn't be. This chapter presents some basic tips on how to judge the quality of a jewelry mounting. (The mounting is the entire metal part of a jewelry piece before the stones are set in it.) If you follow these tips, you'll be more likely to make a wise jewelry choice.

## Selecting a Sturdy Ring or Bangle Bracelet Mounting

No matter how careful a person is with a ring or bracelet, it will get scratched, bumped, and rubbed. Therefore it's important to choose one that can withstand some wear. Jewelry items such as earrings, pins, and tie-tacs can be more fragile.

This section briefly focuses on two subjects related to low durability--very lightweight mountings and hollow centers. Impractical designs, too, have a negative impact on the sturdiness of a mounting, but a detailed discussion of design problems would be too complicated for this book. The detection of weak links in flexible bracelets is also beyond the scope of this book.

**Fig. 5.1** Lightweight rings designed for occasional use, not everyday wear

**Fig. 5.2** A sturdy ring suitable for daily wear.

The easiest way to test the strength of a ring or bangle bracelet (a non-flexible-type bracelet that slips over the hand) is to squeeze it gently in your hand. If it bends or dents, it's not suitable for long-term, everyday wear. Always get permission from the jeweler or salesperson before doing this test. If they won't let you try the squeeze test, then this indicates the piece is probably not very sturdy. Even some jewelers use this test to help them avoid buying flimsy merchandise. They also use it as an object lesson for their customers.

Another test is to gently bounce the mounting in your hand and see how heavy it feels. If it doesn't have a good solid feel, then it's probably either hollow or too thin. Normally the more lightweight a piece is, the less durable it is. Lightweight pieces also cost less since they have less gold. This is why they are promoted so heavily to people looking for bargain prices. Buying mountings that are too thin, however, is shortsighted. The repairs on them later can end up costing more than the pieces themselves.

Even people with lots of money sometimes skimp on the quality of their mountings. For example, they may pay $10,000 for a diamond but be unwilling to spend a little extra to get a ring that will hold the stone securely and provide long-term wear. Gold is usually the least expensive part of a jewelry piece. It's the labor and the gems that normally add the most value to the piece.

Mountings that look big and heavy but feel light are apt to be hollow. It's a good idea to always ask if a piece is hollow. Salespeople should tell you this without being asked, but they don't always do so. Hollow jewelry presents a variety of problems. When the walls of the piece are thin, it dents and wears through quickly, leaving holes. Repairing it is difficult or impossible. Hollow rings are not easy to size. You can avoid a lot of possible distress by buying a solid every-day ring rather than a hollow one.

Hollow bangle bracelets can be sturdy while at the same time being more comfortable than a solid one of the same size. The key is the thickness of the gold. One New York jeweler says he tests his hollow bracelets with the squeeze test, and he invites his customers to do the same. Then they try to dent them with pressure from their fingertips. These sturdy hollow bracelets feel substantial in weight. If you're in the market for a hollow bangle bracelet, you may wish to consider buying one of the twisted metal styles. The multiple ridges makes the bracelet stronger and more rigid, and they help hide any signs of wear.

Jewelers can usually tell just by looking at a piece if it's sturdy. It's harder for laypeople to do this, but even they can easily see the difference between lighter and heavier rings. For example, compare the rings in figures 5.1 and 5.2. When examining the appearance of mountings, keep in mind that cast pieces need to be thicker than die-struck or hand-fabricated ones. This is mainly because cast metal is more porous and less dense.

Stores should be able to give you sound advice on choosing mountings, but this is not always the case. Jewelers or salespeople who only talk price and never mention quality may not know enough about jewelry to help you select good-quality pieces, not to mention the fact that they probably don't insist on quality merchandise from their suppliers. Therefore it's best to deal with knowledgeable people who take pride in the quality of their jewelry.

The ethics of jewelers are also an important consideration. Figure 5.3 shows a thick, solid 18K-gold ring with invisible-set diamonds. As you can see, it's broken. After being set, the ring was placed in a pan of boiling water to clean off the shellac used to hold it during setting. Then the water ran dry. The ring broke when cooled in water. It would have been a lot cheaper and faster to just solder the two pieces together or to

**Fig. 5.3** Repair it or redo it?

add a new shank (bottom part of the ring attached to the stone setting), but the jeweler chose to cast a new ring and reset all of the stones. This was the proper thing to do because the ring was to be sold as a new ring, not a repaired one. In addition, the fact that the ring broke indicated the gold had been structurally weakened. Perhaps the best way for a consumer to avoid buying repaired or defective jewelry, is to deal with a trustworthy jeweler.

Some people have given up on wearing rings because they have large or arthritic knuckles. If they do slip on a ring, it's usually too big and twists around on their fingers. There's a solution to this problem. An adjustable ring shank can be soldered to the bottom half of the ring (see figure 5.4). If the shank has been made to a size 6, for example, it can open to a size 9. For more information on adjustable ring shanks, consult your local jeweler.

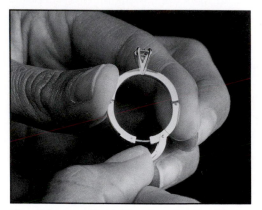

Fig. 5.4 An adjustable ring shank. *Photo courtesy River Gems & Findings*

Fig. 5.5 Unacceptable gold porosity.

## Porosity Problems

It's normal for cast rings to have some **porosity** (air holes). Therefore you shouldn't reject a piece of jewelry just because there are a couple of minor pits. However, large pores or groupings of pits such as the ones in figures 5.5 and 5.6 are unacceptable. Besides detracting from the beauty of the piece, this type of porosity can indicate serious durability problems. Metal with holes in it is naturally weaker than smooth, dense metal. In addition, the more porous a metal is, the lower its polish and luster will be. Improper casting and soldering as well as the use of old gold are the main causes of porosity.

Some people like to cast pieces from gold that consists of remelted broken chains or old jewelry. This saves them money on refining and alloying costs. Unfortunately, scrap gold often contains a lot of impurities and solder, which creates serious porosity in newly cast jewelry. If you are having a piece custom made, have the jeweler use freshly refined gold. The only good reason to use old gold in jewelry is for its sentimental value.

Porosity can be patched with solder and hidden with textured finishes. This may make the piece look better, but it doesn't correct the inherent weakness of the metal itself.

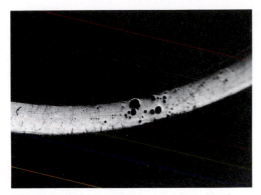

Fig. 5.6  Gold porosity on a ring shank

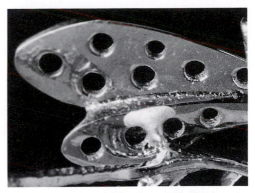

Fig. 5.7  Excess solder in a "T" shape

## Solder Problems

Gold jewelry sometimes falls apart in ultrasonic cleaners. This can happen when it is not properly soldered (joined with a metal that melts at a lower temperature). To be made strong, joined surfaces must be clean, well-aligned and tight-fitting. Proper heating and control of the solder is also required. When jobs are rushed or jewelers are not well-skilled, solder problems can arise. Figure 5.7 is an example of excess solder on an exposed jewelry surface. This piece was delivered as a finished mounting. It's 18K gold and designed to be set with expensive diamonds. Besides looking ugly, visible blobs of solder suggest that the jeweler may have also done a poor job of soldering the joints.

The use of inappropriate solders is another major solder problem. Sometimes lead or silver is used to solder gold. At other times, **low-karat gold solders** are chosen (these solders have a karat value much lower than the metal joined, as low as 6K). It's tempting for a jeweler to use low-karat solders because they cost less and they melt at low temperatures, making it easier for a poorly skilled person to do the soldering.

Listed below are reasons why it's important for the appropriate solder to be used on your jewelry (for example 14K gold solder on a 14K piece):

1. Because this will help prevent the solder joints from tarnishing and discoloring. Gold jewelry that's made with low-karat solder may look good when bought; but after it's worn and comes in contact with perspiration, lotions, cosmetics etc, the solder joints may turn brown because of the high percentage of alloying metals in the solder. Some 14K-gold alloys may darken slightly. However, they should not turn dark brown or green.

2. Because low-karat solders can cause a green, brown, or black residue to form on your skin. This is due to the chemical reaction of the alloying metals with your skin oils and perspiration. For example, low-karat solder in a 14K gold chain may cause a green ring to form around your neck, depending on your body chemistry. Reactions from 14K jewelry with 14K solder have also been reported. However, when jewelry is made with a solder of 10K or lower, the chances are much greater that a residue will appear. In the chapters on determining gold fineness and fake gold, you'll learn that ten-karat gold typically turns dark brown when acid is applied.

3. Because it will be easier to change settings or do repairs on your piece later on. When the author was interviewing jewelers for this book, several complained of how some of the jewelry brought in for repair literally fell apart the moment a torch was used on it. This was because it had been made with low-karat solder which had a very low melting temperature. Low-karat solder is not just being used to join surfaces, it's used to patch holes, fill in wirework, and build up prongs or other parts of the piece. High-quality jewelers, however, do not construct their pieces this way.

4. Because usually a better color match is possible between the gold and the solder when the correct solder is used.

5. Because it's logical for you to expect that a piece marked 14K be made of 14K gold, solder included.

In Britain, jewelers must use the right solder. According to *The Retail Jeweller's Guide* by Kenneth Blakemore (p. 190), "solder has to be the same quality as the metal it joins, because with a few exceptions this is demanded by the hallmarking laws." On page 8 of his book, Blakemore says "Even the solder used by the jewellry trade must pass an assay."

British jewelers must also use the appropriate solder for repairs. In his book *Practical Jewelry Repair* (page 85), James Hickling brings up the problem of soldering a new shank to a head set with heat-sensitive stones that can't be removed or protected. He states that if a customer wants the shank repaired, "the only solution is to use soft (low-karat) solder, but then the ring is legally not gold and must not bear a hallmark, or be sold as gold in the U.K."

In America, the use of low-karat solder has become so widespread that it is almost considered acceptable. Many American jewelers, however, are strongly opposed to this trend. They feel that the routine use of low-karat solders is unethical and lowers the quality of jewelry.

According to American and Canadian regulations, the pure gold content of new jewelry must be within 7 parts per thousand of the stamped karat mark. This means that 18K (750) gold cannot fall below a fineness of 743 even when assayed with the solder. There are no regulations, however, which specify what type of solder must be used. When it comes to sizings and repairs, it's up to the consumers to indicate the type of solder desired. As one official has commented, "it's like going to a restaurant and telling the waitress how you would like your steak cooked." The difference, though, is that jewelry stores don't ask preference questions such as "Would you like your 14K ring sized with silver, lead, 6K, 10K or 14K solder?"

This means that if low-karat solder causes a brown sizing line to form on your ring after it's worn for awhile, then legally it's your fault if you didn't tell the jeweler to use the appropriate solder. When dealing with a reputable jeweler, you needn't worry about this because they automatically use solders that match the gold content of your jewelry (except in a few instances where its use may be warranted). But if, for example, you need an 18K gold ring enlarged and you don't personally know the jeweler who will be doing the sizing, you should have the salesperson write on the take-in form and on your receipt, "Please size ring with 18K solder and 18K gold." (There are some people that even use a lower karat gold stock when enlarging rings.)

Figure 5.8 shows a prong that turned black after it was retipped. In this case, the use of a low-heat, low-karat solder was justified because high heat could cause the opal to crack or discolor. A solution to this would be to take the opal out of the setting, solder on another prong, and reset it. The root of the problem is that the owner of the ring chose a non-durable cluster setting. Tips on choosing a sturdy setting are given in the next chapter.

**Fig. 5.8** Towards the left, a blackened, low-karat gold prong

Some people have given up on wearing gold jewelry because it causes a black smudge to form on their skin. The smudge can be the result of either a chemical or abrasive reaction (make-up and cleansers can act as abrasives). If you've had this problem, try the following:

♦ Switch to a higher karat gold, such as 18 or 22K (In Asia, some people won't buy jewelry that's less than 22K).

♦ Deal with a jeweler who uses the appropriate solders. You may be reacting to the solder, not the karat gold of the mounting. There are lots of jewelers who believe in using the right solder. In fact, some specify that their suppliers give them plumb gold solders--solders that have their full gold content. Otherwise a 14K gold solder, for example, may end up being 12 or 13K.

♦ Plate the piece with 24K gold or with rhodium if it's white gold. Positive results have also been obtained by just rhodium-plating the inside of yellow-gold rings.

♦ Try a different gold alloy. Jewelers who alloy their own metals may help you find a suitable alloy. Your body reacts to the metals the gold is alloyed with (copper or nickel, for example), not the gold itself. Dentists have to choose their gold alloys carefully. As a result, gold crowns don't create a black smudge in the mouth.

## Judging Finish

Many jewelers feel that one of the easiest ways for the layperson to judge craftsmanship is to look at the back of the jewelry piece. If it's well-finished on the back and underneath, chances are it's well constructed. Look at figure 5.9 and note the roughness of the metal. Further examination reveals a lot of porosity, irregular prongs, poorly soldered joints, and excess solder.

Fig. 5.9 A rough unacceptable finish

Fig. 5.10 Cast ring with an average but acceptable finish

Now look at the back of the cast brooch in figure 5.11 and color photos 5a & b. Not only is it cleanly finished, it has an attractive decorative design. The fact that the jeweler could make the back of this piece look as good as the front indicates he has the skill and desire to construct it properly too.

Figure 5.10 is an example of a piece with an average finish. It's not easy to polish the inner curved surfaces of cast jewelry. Even though the interior of this ring is not perfectly smooth, the company that made it eliminated the roughness, making it an acceptable mounting. The ring also feels comfortable when worn.

**Fig. 5.11** High-quality finish on the back of a brooch. *Photo courtesy Forest Jewelers.*

Color photo 5c shows the back of the brooch pictured on the book cover. It took about one hour to clean and prepare it for polishing after casting. Then another 4 to 5 hours were spent polishing it to give it the smooth and shiny inner surface. Knowing how much work is required to do a piece well makes it easier to understand jewelry pricing.

The feel of a jewelry piece is a good indication of the quality of its finish and polish. If the piece has jagged edges, file marks, or sharp points that scratch you or catch on your clothing, it's not well finished. High-quality pieces will have a smooth, polished finish throughout, even in the areas behind the gemstones.

When evaluating jewelry, do not assume that it's of high quality if it is expensive, hand-fabricated, or custom-made. Most of the examples of bad setting in the next chapter are of pieces that have sold for more than $2000. On the other hand, there are a lot of reasonably priced, mass-produced pieces that are sturdy and well-finished. The karat value is not necessarily an indication of quality of workmanship either. Even though it's true that some of the finest jewelry is made with 18K gold, it's not hard to find poorly-made 18K pieces. Lots of 10K jewelry is well crafted. Therefore don't evaluate jewelry on the basis of its price tag or prestige value. Be objective and openminded. This will help you select an attractive, long-wearing piece.

# 6

# Judging the Setting

Some couples will spend a lot of time selecting an engagement diamond, yet they'll neglect to choose a secure setting for it.  Everyday rings get a lot of abuse.  Consequently, they need a strong setting.  This chapter offers some practical tips on selecting one.

## Choosing a Secure Prong (Claw) Setting

The most popular setting style for a diamond solitaire ring is the prong setting (called claw setting in Britain).  This is mainly because it allows the stone to sit higher, making it appear more prominent and lighter than it would in other settings.  The proper prong setting can hold large stones securely for years.  However, some cluster prong settings, such as the ones in figure 5.1 of the last chapter, are notorious for having small stones fall out of them.  This is due to the thinner prongs and to the fact that often less care is taken in setting the smaller stones.  As a result, a cluster setting is not the best choice for an everyday ring which will get lots of wear.

Another term used for the setting is **the head**.  An example of a head and shank (circular part of ring) is shown in figure 6.1.  Sometimes the head is not separate from the shank.  The mounting is just one continuous cast piece of metal.  One-piece mountings require less labor than mountings made of two or more pieces.  Therefore, they tend to cost less.

When choosing an everyday ring such as an engagement ring, you are better off buying a ring that has a separate head soldered to it. If the prongs wear out, the head can easily be replaced--a much better solution than retipping the prongs. In addition, multiple-piece mountings allow you the option of putting in a head with stronger metal than the shank.

**Fig. 6.1** A die-struck head and shank

It was mentioned in the chapter on manufacturing methods that hand-fabricated and die-struck (machine-stamped) prongs can be stronger and of a more consistent thickness than cast prongs. In the chapter on gold colors, data will be provided showing that some white gold and platinum alloys are more durable than typical yellow gold alloys. This means that if a jeweler solders a die-struck platinum head to a cast gold shank, the setting can last a lot longer than if the whole ring were cast as one unit.

Die-struck prong settings are not made for stones of unusual sizes or shapes. There's a much wider selection of cast settings. These cast settings are suitable for mountings that do not receive a great deal of wear (e.g. pendants, pins, earrings, dress rings, tie-tacs). However, if you're looking for maximum durability in an everyday ring, but no die-struck heads are available for it, you'd be better off having a hand-fabricated setting made with wires that have been pulled or compressed. The disadvantage is that a handmade setting will normally cost more than a cast one. There isn't much difference, though, between the price of a die-struck and cast setting.

Normally, mass-produced die-struck and cast settings will have the proper number of prongs for the size of your stone. Some rings which are cast as one unit, however, may not have enough prongs to hold the stone securely. For example, some cluster rings have only one prong holding each of the stones. As a general rule of thumb, solitaire prong settings should have at least four prongs. Large stones need more prongs than small stones. Also, yellow gold settings may require more prongs than white gold or platinum ones. If you are selecting a marquise or pear shape stone, make sure the point(s) are well protected with a prong(s).

In summary, if you are buying an everyday ring with a prong setting and you'd like to wear it for a long time:

♦ Buy a ring that has been constructed with a separate head.

♦ Choose a ring with a die-struck or hand-fabricated setting rather than a cast one.

♦ Make sure the setting has enough prongs to hold the stone securely.

♦ Avoid cluster settings with tiny stones.

# Evaluating a Prong Setting

To adequately judge the quality of a setting, some type of magnifier is needed. ("**Setting**" can refer to the part of a mounting that holds the gemstones or to the way in which the stones have been set.) You can find 5- and 10-power hand magnifiers in coin and stamp shops and some discount stores. They sell for as little as $6 to $15 and are adequate for evaluating gold jewelry. These magnifiers can also be used for other purposes such as reading fine print or examining photo negatives. For grading gems, a 10-power triplet loupe (fig. 6.2) is usually recommended. (A triple lens structure in the loupe helps prevent distortion.) A good loupe will cost at least $25. People accustomed to using a loupe like to also use it for checking the setting and the quality of the mounting.

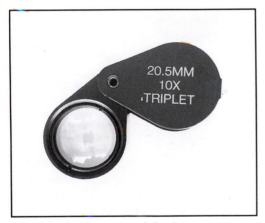

**Fig. 6.2** A 10-power triplet loupe

**Fig. 6.3** Note the space between the center stone and the left and right prongs. These prongs are not supporting the stone.

Before you go shopping, it's a good idea to practice using your magnifier on some jewelry that you already own. Listed below are points you should consider when judging the quality of a prong setting.

**The prongs**  **Are the prongs in contact with the stone?** If they aren't, that means they are not holding the stone. To detect space between the prongs and the stone, you usually have to look at the setting from the side. Figure 6.3 is an example of prongs not supporting a stone.

Another way to detect space between a stone and a prong is to try to slide a piece of paper between them. The paper won't pass if the prong is holding the stone properly. This test is particularly effective for checking solitaire settings.

**Do the prongs look too thin or too thick?** Figure 6.4 illustrates prongs that are too bulky looking. Prongs should have enough metal to hold the stone securely but not so much that they hide its beauty. Figures 6.6 and 6.7 are examples of acceptable prongs.

**Do the prongs have porosity (air holes)?** If they do, this indicates they are weak. The tall prong to the left in figure 6.3 shows some of the porosity in this setting. A lot more holes are visible from other angles. The person who worked on this setting built it up with solder and then created a lot of porosity by overheating the solder. Prongs like these can break easily.

**Do the prongs have rough or sharp edges?** If so, the prongs can snag your clothes or scratch you. Prongs can also catch on fabric when they are not set tight against the stone.

**Are any of the prongs or prong tips missing?** If they are, the piece may be secondhand. Otherwise, it's the result of poor casting or setting. If the prongs are missing from jewelry you own, get them repaired before a stone falls out.

**Are the shape and size of the prongs consistent?** There are lots of good prong styles. Once the setter has chosen one for a setting, he should stick to it. Prongs don't have to be perfectly formed or exactly the same to be acceptable (there will always be a little variation). However, when they vary as much as the ones in figure 6.5, this is considered low-quality setting.

Sometimes a poor casting is the cause of prongs of odd sizes and shapes. Look at the prongs of the mounting in figure 6.8. No matter how skilled a setter were, he'd have a hard time doing high quality setting on this piece. Figure 6.9 shows how a bad casting combined with poor setting can result in irregular, bulky prongs.

Irregular prongs can be secure, but they are aesthetically unattractive and they indicate other more serious problems may be present.

**The head**    **Is the head soldered securely to the shank?** Sometimes the head is attached only at a small point instead of being soldered flat against surfaces of the shank. If the joints don't fit well, they won't be as strong as they should be.

**Fig. 6.4** Bulky-looking prongs

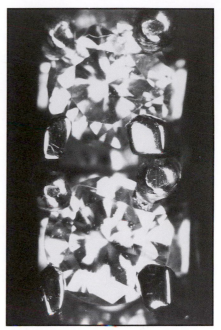

**Fig. 6.5** Irregular prongs

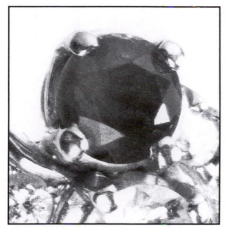

**Fig. 6.6** An acceptable prong setting

**Fig. 6.7** A platinum setting that has secured a diamond during 50 years of constant wear. It's never been repaired.

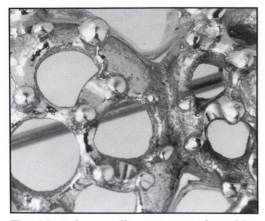

**Fig. 6.8** A low-quality cast mounting with irregular prongs

**Fig. 6.9** Bulky irregular prongs of a poorly cast mounting

**Is the head on straight?** Crooked heads detract from the appearance of the piece and they may indicate that the head isn't attached securely to the shank.

**Is the head too big or too small for the stone?** This is easier for a jeweler to judge, but even the layperson can tell when the head is obviously out of proportion to the stone. It's not uncommon to see heads that are too small. Besides looking out of balance, they don't secure the stone properly.

**The stone(s)**  **Are any of the stones chipped?** It's not unusual for poorly skilled setters to chip stones when trying so secure them tightly. Sometimes they just leave the stones in the setting and try to cover up the chip with a prong. If you spot a chipped stone, ask to have it replaced if there are no other quality problems, Otherwise choose another piece.

**Are the stones level?** Lopsided stones look out of balance and are unable to display maximum brilliance. They also suggest the presence of other craftsmanship deficiencies.

**Are the stones matched?** Poor matching does not affect durability, but it's aesthetically unpleasing. Keep in mind that no two gems are exactly alike. Therefore they will never match perfectly. The stones should, however, blend together well. If you ever lose one of the stones in a setting, it may be difficult or impossible for a jeweler to find a good match to replace it. This is another reason to make sure your stones are securely set.

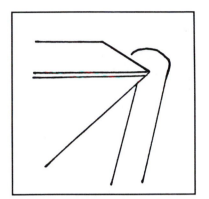

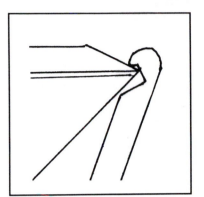

**Fig. 6.10**  Edge of stone flat against the seat in the prong

**Fig. 6.11**  Poorly seated stone

**The seat**   **Is there a seat for the stone in the prongs?**  (The seat is a notch or groove in the prong which supports the stone.  It's also called **the bearing**.)  Setters use a cone-shaped drill called a bur to form the seat.  Occasionally they just bend over the prongs and neglect to put in a seat.  A stone without a seat is not secure.

**Is the stone set securely in the seat?**  The outside edges of the stone should be flat against the seat as in figure 6.10.  Otherwise the stone will not be stable and well-supported.  Figures 6.3 and 6.11 are examples of improperly made seats not securing a stone.

## Evaluating Channel Setting

In this style, stones are lined up in a channel formed by two metal walls (fig. 6.12)  No metal separates the stones, but there may be bars underneath acting as supports.  When done properly, channel setting holds small stones more securely than prongs.  It protects the girdle area (outer edge) of the stones and it provides a smoother and lower surface than prongs.

One disadvantage is that it's more time consuming than prong setting.  Consequently, it's more expensive.  Diamonds and rubies are frequently channel set, but fragile stones such as opal or topaz are not suited for this style.  This setting process can easily cause them to chip and crack.

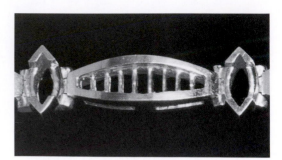

Fig. 6.13 Note the bars in this channel bracelet mounting.

Fig. 6.12 High quality channel setting. *Photo courtesy Levine Design.*

It can be hard to determine if a stone is well-seated in a channel setting. This is because the seat may not be visible. However, if an evaluation of the following points is positive, chances are the stone is securely seated.

**The channel(s)** **Is metal securing both ends of the stones?** If not, there's a risk of losing the stones.

**Do the walls (sides) of the channels look thick enough to support the stones?** If the mounting feels unusually light or looks like you could bend it, the walls are probably too thin.

**Are there any metal bars supporting the stones from behind?** When bars are placed at intervals behind the stones, they can prevent a widening of the channel and the consequent loss of stones. The longer the channel, the more important bars become. Figure 6.13 shows a mounting with supporting bars.

**Has the inside and back of the channel been polished?** Rough dull surfaces can reflect in the stones, keeping them from looking as brilliant as possible. A high-quality finish is a sign of high-quality setting.

**Are the edges of the channel(s) even and smooth?** Rough, wavy edges like the ones in figure 6.14 look bad and indicate poor setting.

**Does metal cover too much of the stone?** Even though there needs to be enough metal to secure the stone, as much of the stone as possible should be visible. Too much metal is covering the stone on the left in figure 6.15.

**Fig. 6.14**  Crooked, poorly secured stones in a very porous mounting

**Fig. 6.15**  Partially hidden stone in a channel setting

**The stones**    **Are any of the stones chipped?**  It's common to find chipped stones in channel-set pieces.  Therefore, check for this carefully.

**Are any of the stones crooked?** (fig. 6.14)  If so, this indicates they may be improperly seated in the mounting.  Crooked stones also detract from the appearance of the piece.

**Are the stones level?**  The surface across the stones should be flat.  This allows them to display their maximum brilliance and makes the piece more attractive.

**Are the stones overlapping**.  Stones that overlap, are susceptible to chipping, especially if the piece is accidentally knocked against furniture or walls.

**Are the stones poorly matched?**  If there are obvious, distracting differences in the color, cut proportions, and/or clarity of the stones, they are considered to be poorly matched.  Normally, there will be minor variations, but these shouldn't keep you from buying a piece.

Channel mountings are frequently set with squares and **baguettes** (square-cornered, rectangular stones).  These are more difficult to match than round stones because there are so many more sizes to choose from.  The larger and more unusual the size of the stone, the harder it is to match.  Well-matched natural ruby or diamond baguettes may sell at a premium due to the amount of time required to find stones of the same size, proportioning, and color.  A good way to gain an appreciation for well-matched baguettes is to spend a few hours trying to match them.

# Pavé and Bezel setting

Pavé setting involves placing stones into holes of a mounting and then forming beads (small prongs) from the surrounding metal to hold them in place.  Figure 6.16 is an example of a pavé-set piece.  The finished surface looks like it's been paved with stones, hence the French name "pavé."  An example of a pavé mounting before setting is shown in figure 6.17.  Pavé setting is mainly used in women's jewelry.  This style of setting is best suited for creating surface designs or brilliance on pins, necklaces, and earrings.  It's impractical for everyday rings because the beads tend to wear down causing stones to fall out.  The smaller the stones are, the greater the risk of loss.

Bezel setting (figure 6.18) is a popular style for both men's and women's jewelry.  A band of metal (called a bezel) is pressed around the edge of the stone to hold it in place.  The bezel protects the edge of the stone and provides a secure setting for stones subjected to a lot of wear.

**Fig. 6.16** The pavé-set diamonds in this brooch add sparkle to broad surface areas of the piece.

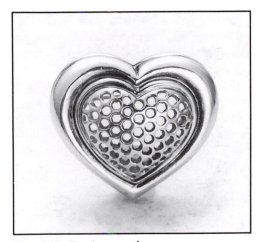

**Fig. 6.17** Pavé mounting

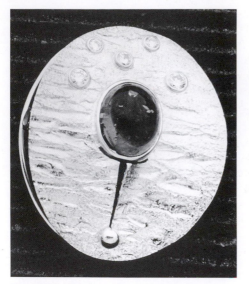

A few tips on evaluating pavé and bezel settings are briefly listed below.

♦ Verify that all the stones are secured by metal.
♦ Make sure no stones have been scraped or chipped.
♦ Examine the back of the mounting to see if it's been finished well.
♦ Check if the edge of the bezel is smooth and even or if the small prongs are uniform and well-shaped.
♦ Make a judgement about the overall aesthetic appearance of the piece.

**Fig. 6.18** High-quality bezel setting. *Photo courtesy Richard Kimball.*

# Miscellaneous Tips

♦ **When you go to bed, either take your ring(s) off or turn them towards your palm.** While sleeping, you probably unconsciously hit your rings against the sheets. The dust on the sheets or the fabric itself acts as a fine abrasive, which over a period of time can wear down the setting. The palm of your hand is less likely to rub against the sheets than the outer part.

♦ **When possible, take off your jewelry when engaging in contact sports or when doing housework, yard work and other chores**. This will prevent abnormal wear. While jewelry is made of metal and stone, it's not indestructible. Even diamonds can be inadvertently chipped and cracked when subjected to knocks and unusual stress.

♦ **When choosing a ring style, consider your lifestyle, how often you'll wear it, and how you tend to use your hands.** This can have a great bearing on what style may be most appropriate for you.

♦ **Keep in mind that eternity rings can be difficult or impossible to size, especially if they are channel set.** Before buying a ring with stones going part way or all the way around the mounting, ask if there will be a problem sizing it. Even if the ring fits at the time of purchase, it may not fit later on if you gain or lose weight.

♦ **Buy secure settings and mountings instead of promotional "life-time guarantees."** Even though some warranties are offered for legitimate reasons, many industries also like to use them as a gimmick to make their product appear more desirable than it actually is. For example, a 20-year warranty on a mattress does not necessarily mean it will last 20 years. It usually indicates that if the mattress wears out in say 10 years, the company will give you a 50% discount on a new one. In other words, it's a prorated guarantee.

Similarly, a lifetime warranty on a piece of jewelry is no guarantee that it will last a lifetime. Lots of flimsy rings have been sold with lifetime guarantees. Most guarantees against stone loss usually require the buyer to return to the store every four to six months to have the setting checked. It's easy to forget to do this and invalidate the guarantee. Another potential problem is that the store may try to avoid replacing the stone by claiming it fell out due to abnormal wear.

If you buy sturdy jewelry from a reputable jeweler, you won't need to be concerned about a warranty. A lot of jewelers automatically back their merchandise even without a written guarantee. Naturally, though, the buyer must be willing to select a long-wearing piece as well as avoid abnormal abuse such as slamming the piece in a doorjamb or dropping it in a garbage disposal.

♦ **Every month or so, shake your jewelry next to your ear and check if it rattles.** If it does, a stone is probably loose and needs to be fixed right away. It's a good idea to have a professional look at your jewelry about every six months if you wear it often. They can spot problems you may miss.

# Quiz (Chapters 5 & 6)

## True or false?

1. Jewelry cast from scrap gold tends to be more porous and less durable than that which is made from freshly refined gold.

2. 18K jewelry is sturdier than 14K jewelry.

3. Channel-set stones should overlap slightly so no space shows between them.

4. If a jewelry piece has a lifetime guarantee, it will last a lifetime.

5. If a stone is set with enough prongs of the proper size, then it will be held securely.

6. The finish on the back of a piece provides important clues about its overall quality.

7. Rings with small pavé-set diamonds are ideal for everyday wear.

8. If a jewelry piece has scratches, it's of poor quality.

9. Your ring prongs can undergo wear while you are sleeping.

10. When having jewelry repaired, sized, or custom-made, it's a good idea to specify that the appropriate solder be used if you don't personally know who will be working on your piece.

11. Hollow rings are a good option for men on limited budgets.

12. A ring that is cast as one unit will provide longer wear than one which is assembled.

13. Eternity rings can be difficult or impossible to size.

14. Machine-stamped prongs are not as durable as cast prongs.

15. Bracelet and ring mountings need to be sturdier than earring and brooch mountings.

## Answers:

1. **T**

2. **F**

3. **F**   Overlapping stones are very susceptible to chipping.

4. **F**

5. **F**   Other factors are also important.  A major problem with a lot of mass-produced jewelry is that the stones in it are not well seated or have no seat at all.

6. **T**

7. **F**

8. **F**   Since gold scratches easily, well-made pieces get scratched.  Therefore, you shouldn't reject a piece on the basis of a few scratches.  Just have the jeweler polish them away.

9. **T**

10. **T**

11. **F**   The walls of an inexpensive hollow ring are likely to be too thin to provide long-term wear.  Also, hollow jewelry tends to cost more per gram than sturdy, solid jewelry.

12. **F**

13. **T**

14. **F**   They are **more** durable than cast prongs.

15. **T**

# 7

# Gold Chains

## Rope Chain

**Fig. 7.1** Which rope chain costs more? Each is 14K gold, 16 inches long. and machine-made.

To answer this question correctly, you also need to know the weight of the chains. The thinner chain (2.5mm) weighs 8.6 grams. The thicker chain (3mm) weighs 4.8 grams because it is hollow. Although its cost per gram is slightly more, its total cost is much less than the thinner solid chain.

The advantages and disadvantages of solid and hollow rope chains are as follows:

## Advantages of solid rope chain:

♦ It's sturdy, especially compared to hollow rope chain and flat chains like the herringbone. The thicker the chain, the stronger it is.

♦ It's ideal for suspending pendants and charms. However, the heavier the pendant, the thicker the chain should be. Good salespeople will be able to help you select a chain of an appropriate thickness if you show them the type of pendant(s) you plan to wear on the chain.

♦ For Americans, its price per gram is often a little less than other types of chain. This is because so much of it is produced domestically and has no import duties levied on it.

## Disadvantages of solid rope chain:

♦ Even though it can be repaired to look like new, it's not as easy to repair as a solid link chain. Hand-made rope however is easier to repair than the machine-made type.

## Advantages of hollow rope chain:

♦ It's lighter weight than solid chain and therefore more comfortable.

♦ It costs almost half the price of solid chain of the same width.

## Disadvantages of hollow rope chain:

♦ Even though it can be repaired, it may not look like new afterwards. If there's a hole or break at one point of the chain, there is likely to be a weakness elsewhere. Repairs can become a never-ending process with hollow chains of any style.

♦ It's not a good chain for suspending heavy pendants or charms. The friction of the pendant wears down the thin metal wall, and the chain breaks. Some hollow chains come with a lifetime guarantee, but the guarantee does not cover loss or damage to a pendant when the chain breaks. If the receipt is lost or misplaced, the guarantee may not be valid.

♦ It's a poor choice for a bracelet. The banging and knocks that occur on the wrist can dent the chain.

♦ Its price per gram is usually a bit higher than solid rope.

Salespeople are supposed to tell you if a chain is hollow. Some, however, may be unaware of the hollow center or else afraid of losing the sale if they disclose this. A lightweight feel or advertising terms such as **"semi-solid"** and **"50% lighter"** are signals that a chain is hollow.

## Diamond-Cut Rope

Note the tiny flat surfaces on the upper chain in figure 7.2. These reflect light like the facets of a gemstone and give the chain a brighter look. The process of cutting these surfaces is called **diamond cutting**. Since diamond-cut rope sparkles more than standard rope, it tends to sell better.

Some jewelers have had customers complain that diamond-cut rope snags their clothes. Other

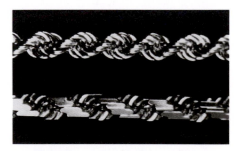

**Fig. 7.2** Top--standard rope, bottom--diamond-cut rope

jewelers say their customers are pleased with it. The cause of this discrepancy is probably that the chains were made by different companies. Some manufacturers do a poor finishing job and leave rough surface edges whereas others give it a high-quality finish. Part of the problem may be the use of old instead of new diamonds to cut the facets. When buying diamond-cut rope, brush it against your clothing and run it lightly through your fingers to see if it snags or scratches. This will help you determine if it's well-finished or not.

## Handmade Rope

Considering its complexity, handmade rope is relatively inexpensive. In fact, in the United States, some high-quality domestic handmade rope sells for a bit less per gram than some Italian machine-made rope. It only takes about an hour for a skilled rope maker to assemble links into an 18", 3mm rope (It takes about 2 hours to make an 18" inch 1mm rope). Additional time is required to solder and finish the rope.

There are various qualities of handmade rope. A high-quality 14K rope will have:

♦ a flexible, tight weave, giving it strength
♦ a smooth, well-finished surface
♦ links of 14K plumb gold (not 13K or 13.5K)
♦ 14K solder instead of a low-karat solder

A good way to compare the weave is to twist the rope slightly. A loosely assembled rope will untwist to a longer length than one which is tighter.

Figure 7.3 is a close-up view of two 3mm handmade chains. They are both 18 inches long, but the top one weighs 14.22 grams and the bottom one 16.6. Note how the loop on the upper rope is more extended and how the background shows through more. The extra spread means the top chain has less gold per inch, less weight and less strength.

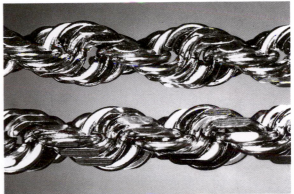

Fig. 7.3 Two handmade ropes magnified. The lower one is more tightly assembled and therefore stronger.

The bottom chain was made in Anaheim, California and the lower one in a country where labor costs are much lower, so one would expect a price difference. However, they are selling for the same price per gram. Due to its lighter weight, though, the top chain would cost less and appear to be a better buy. In reality, it's less quality for the money.

# Flat Chain

The most popular flat chain on the market is the herringbone (figs 7.4 and 7.5). Some jewelers, however, won't stock it because it kinks so easily. Its positive and negative points are listed below:

**Fig. 7.4** Herringbone chain

**Fig. 7.5** Textured and patterned herringbone

## Advantages of herringbone chain

♦ It offers a big look at a low price. The flatness of the chain makes it wider than other types of chain of the same weight and price.

♦ It often looks shinier than rope and link chain. This is due to the light reflecting off of a broader surface area.

♦ It's available in a wide variety of styles and finishes.

## Disadvantages of herringbone chain

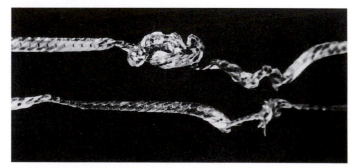

**Fig. 7.6** Kinking. The problem with herringbone chain.

♦ It's not durable (fig. 7.6). Generally, the more lightweight it is, the more likely it is to kink or break. Yet manufacturers are making them thinner and thinner. Some of the more flexible or heavier styles may be less likely to kink.

♦ It's not a good chain for pendants.

♦ It's hard to repair it properly. The mended part may be rigid.

When interviewing jewelers and chain dealers for this book, the author did not find one who recommended this chain. The overall consensus was why buy a herringbone chain when there are so many better ones to choose from.

In general, flat chains don't last as well as solid link and rope chains, and repairing them may be a problem. Some of the thicker ones such as the **omega** (fig. 7.7) do wear better than the herringbone. Several jewelers mentioned that the **serpentine (s-chain)** has a tendency to kink. In fairness to the serpentine chain, the one in figure 7.8 has been worn by the owner day and night for over 15 years and is still in good condition. As with any chain, the thickness has a lot to do with its durability.

**Fig. 7.7**  Omega chain

**Fig. 7.8**  Serpentine or S-chain

## Link Chain

Solid-link chains get the highest ratings from jewelers and chain dealers alike. Link chains come in a wide variety of styles. One that is particularly popular now is the **anchor chain** (fig. 7.9). Verbally, it is often referred to as the **Gucci chain**, but this an infringement of the Gucci trademark. Another popular link chain is the **figaro**. It usually has an alternating pattern of one large and three small links (it can also have patters of 1-2, 1-4, etc.. Sometimes the alternating pattern is combined with other chain styles (fig. 7.11).

Link chains also come in a variety of sizes-- from the small, basic chain termed **cable** (fig. 7.23, second chain from top) to striking jumbo necklaces and bracelets . Cable chain is commonly used for small pendants. Normally the thicker the link the stronger it is, provided it is solid and well-soldered. A link chain that has been twisted about 85° and then flattened is often called a **curb link** (fig 7.10).

**Fig. 7.9  Flat anchor chain**

**Fig. 7.10  Curb link chain**

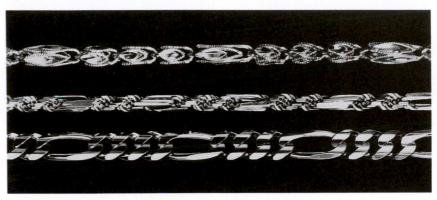

**Fig. 7.11  Top--figaro marquis, center--figarope, bottom--figaro**

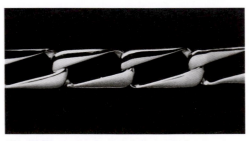

**Fig. 7.12  A basic open link chain**

**Fig. 7.13  Box chain magnified 10 X**

## Advantages of solid link chain

♦ It's strong.

♦ It's a good chain for pendants. Some styles are more suited to this than others.

♦ It's easy to repair to its original state.

♦ It's flexible and hangs nicely.

## Disadvantages of solid link chain

♦ It generally costs more than herringbone chain of the same width because it weighs more.

♦ It's usually not as flashy as herringbone chain.

# Box chain

Most of the box chain on the market is relatively small and lightweight. As its name indicates, this chain looks like a line of little boxes linked together (fig. 7.13). It's most frequently used for hanging charms and small pendants. Naturally, the thicker the box link is, the stronger the chain will be.

Due to its flat surfaces which reflect light, box chain may look brighter than some other small chains. Another advantage is that it doesn't knot as easily as some cable chain. It can also be repaired. Box chain can break if it's very thin, and some of it does not allow pendants to roll as easily as a rope or cable chain.

# Fancy Chain

Unusual chains that look like bracelets and necklaces are often referred to as **fancy chains**. The die-striking (stamping) process by which they are frequently made, allows them to have a very bright polish. Two of the many styles that are currently being sold are the **San Marco** (fig. 7.14) and the **hugs and kisses** (fig. 7.15).

Fancy chain is typically hollow and designed for dress, rather than rough, every-day wear. Special care is required to prevent it from denting and scratching. (Repairing the dents may be impossible.) Its price per gram is generally a bit higher than that of other chains. Since fancy chain is usually hollow and has a big look for its weight, the consumer may think it's less expensive.

**Fig. 7.14** San Marco

**Fig. 7.15** Kisses and hugs

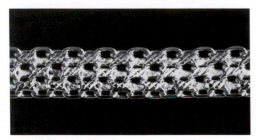

**Fig. 7.16** Bismarck

**Fig. 7.17** Close-up view of Singapore chain

**Fig. 7.18** Singapore chain with mabe pearl pendant

# Miscellaneous Chain

Some chains don't fit well into any of the categories listed above so this book refers to them as miscellaneous. (The jewelry industry does not have a standardized system for classifying chain). The **bismarck** is one example (fig. 7.16). It's made by placing two or more link chains parallel and soldering them together. Another is the **Singapore** chain (fig. 7.17-18).

Several jewelers listed the Singapore as one of the strongest lightweight chains on the market. A close-up view shows that it's essentially a twisted double curb-link chain (fig. 7.17). Naturally the thinner the chain, the more susceptible it is to breaking. The Singapore can be repaired and for the most part, is well-suited for small pendants (7.18).

# Gold-Chain Pricing

Most of the chain sold on the market is machine made and priced by weight--usually the gram, even in the US. (If it were custom-made, it would most likely be priced by the piece.) At the wholesale level, the price changes daily according to the market price of gold. The labor and profit margin must also be figured in.

Often the smaller the chain is, the more it costs per gram. This is because it requires more labor. Nevertheless, pricing systems vary according to the dealer and type of chain. For example, one dealer may decrease its gram prices for rope chain as the width increases. Another dealer may charge slightly more for 4mm rope chain than 3mm. Both would normally charge more per gram for 1mm than 3mm rope chain.

Signs saying "Gold chains, 50% off," are meaningless. At the wholesale level, there is no set price for gold chain. There's only a set price for gold and that can change daily. Any retailer can determine the price they need to charge for chain, double it, and then offer you 50% off.

When shopping, compare chain prices not discount percentages. Make sure that you compare chains of the same weight, style, width, and karat quality. All these factors affect the price. Some stores prefer to sell 10K because they can sell it for less than 14K and still make more. Their customers rarely ask about the karat value and assume they are getting a bargain.

Sometimes salespeople may try to lead you to believe that an 18K or 24K gold-plated chain is more valuable than a 14K solid gold chain. Gold-plated or bonded chain is not gold and it's not worth anywhere near the price of gold. That's why it can be offered at what may seem to be an incredibly low price. If you are looking for real karat-gold jewelry, beware of prices that seem too good to be true. There's probably a catch somewhere.

# Chain Clasps

When buying chains, it's important that you check the clasp and know how it works. It may be defective or hard to open. Ask the salesperson to show you how to open and close it. Then try it twice yourself.

Check that you hear a click when you close the safety lock. Then pull lightly on the chain to verify that the clasp is secure. If you plan to hang a pendant on the chain, make sure that it will fit over the clasp. If it doesn't, the clasp can be changed. Inspect the clasp periodically, and when there's a problem, have it fixed before the clasp comes loose while you're wearing the chain.

**Fig. 7.19**  Spring ring

As you shop for chains, you'll notice they come with a variety of clasps. The main ones are listed below.

♦ **Spring ring** (fig. 7.19). This is a popular clasp for lightweight chains such as the box, cable or Singapore. It's the lowest priced clasp, but perhaps the least secure.

♦ **Barrel clasp (tube or cylinder clasp)** (fig. 7.20). Rope chains often come with barrel clasps. Sometimes people have a hard time determining how to open them and in the process damage the clasp. Be sure to try it a couple times in the store with the help of the salesperson. Occasionally these clasps come loose. Therefore, remember to close the safety lock.

**Fig. 7.20**  Barrel clasp

♦ **Lobster clasp** or **lobster claw** (fig. 7.21). This clasp is frequently seen on the wider herringbone, bismarck and link chains. On a light chain it may look a little heavy, although it's made in different sizes. Many jewelers think it's the most secure clasp for a chain. It's also easy for someone with arthritis to open. The only drawback is its higher cost.

♦ **Box clasp** (fig. 7.22). Fancy chains often have built-in box clasps, which work like the barrel clasp. They can be tailored to the piece and may appear invisible from the top. Sometimes it's hard to find where to open the clasp, so be sure you try it out in the store.

If you are not satisfied with the clasp on a chain you like, keep in mind the clasp can be changed. For extra security, safety chains can be added.

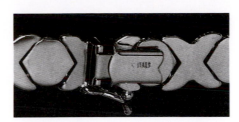

**Fig. 7.21** Lobster clasp

**Fig. 7.22** Back side of a box clasp

## A Practical Lesson in Choosing Chains that Last

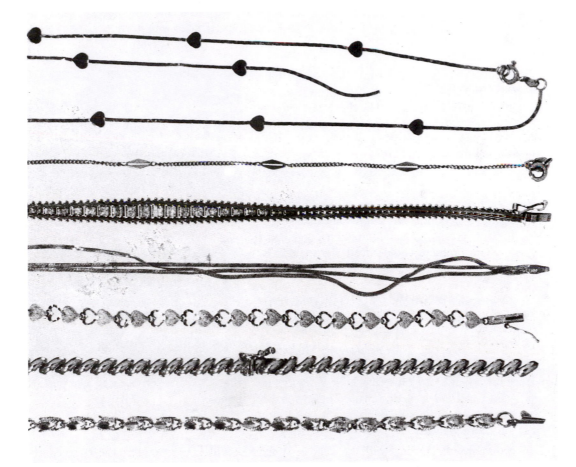

**Fig. 7.23** Which five chains have problems? How could they have been avoided?

The chains pictured in figure 7.23 belong to a friend of the author. The friend, who will be called Mrs. Smith, knew the author was writing a book about gold jewelry and thought the chains might be of interest. A study of Mrs. Smith's experiences can help us avoid the problems she has had. A brief account of each of the above chains is provided below. (The chains are all 14K gold except for the 10K marquis rope bracelet.)

1. **Cobra necklace** (top chain). This chain broke five months after Mrs. Smith received it as a gift. Like the herringbone, the cobra has a tendency to kink and break. Even though this chain can be easily repaired, another type chain such as a link or rope would be much stronger.

2. **Cable bracelet** (2nd from top). There's no problem with this chain. Sometimes thin cable like this one does break, but Mrs. Smith has not had any trouble with it, other than it knots easily.

3. **Fancy bracelet** (3rd from top). The only thing wrong with this bracelet is that the prongs on the edge snag Mrs. Smith's clothes (fig 7.24). Nevertheless, the problem is bad enough that Mrs. Smith no longer wears the bracelet. When you buy rings and bracelets, it's a good idea to brush them against your clothing to check for snagging.

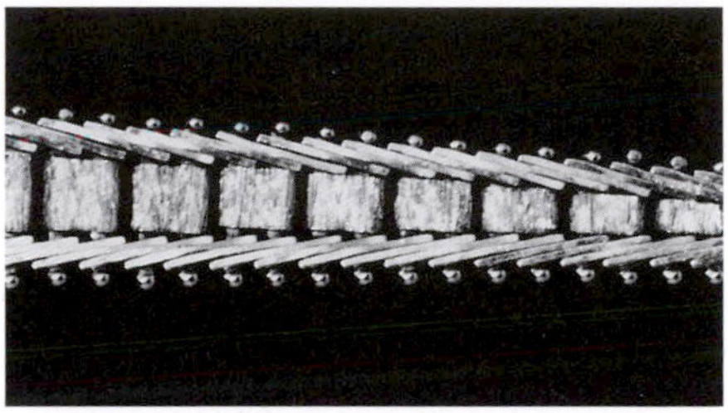

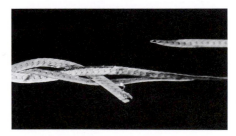

**Fig. 7.24** Prongs on bracelet edge which catch on clothing

4. **Braided herringbone** (4th from top). This chain broke about 2 months after Mrs. Smith got it (fig. 7.25). If it is repaired, it will probably come apart again. The problem could have been avoided by purchasing another type of chain.

5. **Heart bracelet** (5th from top). This is the other chain that has no problem. It's solid and flexible.

6. **San Marco bracelet** (6th from top). This chain broke two weeks after it was bought at a discount store for about $120. Since it is hollow, there's no point in repairing it. The repaired link probably wouldn't hold and another link might break in a couple more weeks.

**Fig. 7.25** Broken braided herringbone

The San Marco was designed for dress. It makes an attractive necklace but is unsuitable for an everyday bracelet, which gets knocked and scraped. Besides breaking easily, the San

Marco also dents and scratches. Mrs. Smith could have avoided wasting $120 by selecting a more durable bracelet.

7. **Marquis rope** (bottom). The clasp comes loose and the chain falls off the wrist. Note how the knob on the safety catch of this bracelet is too small for the catch (fig. 7.26). The knob can easily be enlarged, but Mrs. Smith will still lose a little time and money in the process. Fortunately, she hasn't lost the bracelet. The problem could have been avoided if the person that bought this chain for Mrs. Smith had checked the clasp at the time of purchase.

**Fig. 7.26** Safety catch with too small of a knob

## Why are Chains that Kink and Break so Popular?

The author's survey of jewelers and consumers indicated that the two chain types with the most durability problems were the herringbone and any style of hollow chain. Yet showcases are filled with these chains.

Considering how candid jewelers and chain importers are about the limitations of these chains, one may wonder why they're so popular. It's because their lower prices and bigger look have high sales appeal. And some of the stores promoting them are not fully aware of their low durability.

The buyers for mass merchandisers may have little or no contact with customers. They look at financial reports which show cheap chains usually sell best. It's their job to bring profits to their company by providing their clientele with what it wants. Naturally, they're also interested in customer satisfaction. However, people who buy from mass merchandisers normally don't provide them with feedback by returning damaged chains. Some of the reasons for this are:

♦ People may not have time to go through the hassle of a return.

♦ They may lose the receipt or throw it away since they assume the chain will last.

♦ They may believe it's all their fault if a chain breaks.

♦ The chain may be a gift.

♦ They may be embarrassed they bought such a chain.

◆ There may be no warranty. Some stores don't guarantee chains, even though they guarantee other jewelry.

◆ The warranty period may have expired. (On chains, this period may be less than a month. Occasionally, manufacturers offer lifetime guarantees on non-durable chains. They know most people won't return them if they break.)

Jewelers who actually do repair work on chains and deal directly with their customers are the most adamantly opposed to hollow and herringbone chains. This is no coincidence. They are the ones who have to handle the complaints and explain to customers that these chains may kink or break right after they're repaired.

It's not deceptive for stores to sell non-durable chains. Hollow centers, though, should be disclosed. A good salesperson will advise customers that delicate chains require special care and will suggest a more durable chain as an alternative. It's the consumer's responsibility to heed the advice.

Chains are not destined to break. If your goal is to buy a chain that will last, mention this to the salesperson and be willing to spend a little more on a heavier chain. The long wear you get and the problems you avoid will more than make up for the additional cost.

# Chapter 7 Quiz

Multiple choice

1.  Which chain is most likely to kink?
    a. Rope
    b. Herringbone
    3. Box
    4. Link

2.  Which chain is the hardest to repair properly?
    a. Hollow rope
    b. Curb link
    c. Box
    d. Singapore

3. Which advertising slogan suggests that a chain may not be very strong.
    a. 50% lighter
    b. Soft as silk
    c. Double the width at half the cost
    d. All of the above

4, Which of the following clasps is noted for being secure yet very easy to open.
    a. Spring ring
    b. Barrel clasp
    c. Lobster clasp
    d. Box clasp

5.  When selecting a chain for a pendant you should take into consideration
    a. The size of the pendant
    b. The weight of the pendant
    c. Whether the clasp fits through the pendant bail (suspension loop).
    d. All of the above

## True or False

6.  A chain 1 mm wide would tend to cost more per gram than a 3-mm chain of the same style and quality.

7.  Hollow rope chains tend to cost more per gram than solid rope chains.

8. When buying a chain, it's a good idea to pass it lightly through your fingers to check if there are rough edges which could snag your clothes or scratch you.

9. A chain that is marked at 50% off is probably being sold at a wholesale price.

10. A good chain is typically flexible, comfortable, durable, and easy to repair.

## Answers

1. b

2. a

3, d  The lighter, softer, and thinner a chain is, the more likely it is to break.

4. c

5. d

6. T

7. T

8. T

9. F  You may even discover that in some cases it would be selling for a lot more than the average retail price.

10. T

# 8

# Real Gold or Fake?

Imagine that you have just inherited a large box of jewelry from a relative. You'd like to know if any of it is real gold. This could be determined with the following tests:

## Tests That Require No Acids

**Magnet Test**

Hold a magnet next to the jewelry and see if there is an attraction (fig. 8.1). Gold is not magnetic, but iron and some stainless steel is. When you have a lot of jewelry to check, this can be a quick and effective way of sorting out gold-plated pieces and chains having a base metal of iron or stainless steel.

Magnets can be purchased at toy or hardware stores. Some of the refrigerator magnets are too weak to give reliable results for this test, but some will work.

**Fig. 8.1** Magnet test

**Heaviness Test**

Bounce the jewelry piece in your hand. If it feels unusually light, it's probably not gold. To learn how gold should feel, bounce some in one hand and then compare it to a piece of costume jewelry in the other hand. Keep in mind that hollow gold jewelry or chains may feel like imitation gold.

It will be easier to compare and identify metals by their weight if you know their **specific gravity** (their weight compared to the weight of an equal volume of water. For example, the specific gravity of pure gold is 19.36, meaning it is 19.36 times heavier than water.) Listed below are the specific gravities of some of the metals used to make fine and fashion jewelry. (The main source of this data is *The Retail Jeweller's Guide*, p. 398, by Kenneth Blakemore.)

| | |
|---|---|
| Iridium | 22.41 |
| Platinum | 21.40 |
| Gold (pure) | 19.36 |
| 22K yellow | 17.70 |
| 18K yellow | 15.58 |
| 14K yellow | 13.40 |
| 9K yellow | 11.30 |
| Palladium | 12.00 |
| Silver | 10.53 |
| Copper | 8.94 |
| Nickel | 8.80 |
| Brass | 8.50 |
| Iron | 7.90 |
| Stainless Steel | 7.80 |

**Karat Stamp Test**  Look for a karat or fineness mark on the piece with a hand magnifier (figs. 8.2 - 8.7} (One that is either 5- or 10-power will work. Some marks are even readable with the naked eye.)  The karat stamp is only an indication of the gold content, not proof. On the other hand, the lack of a mark doesn't necessarily mean the piece is not gold.

Occasionally 18K gold is unintentionally stamped 10K and vice versa because the stamps may look so similar.

Gold chains will typically have a karat stamp on the clasp and on a separate plate or link attached to the chain. Sometimes the clasp is plated, but the chain is gold or vice versa. The various components of gold earrings tend to have their own separate marks too. A professional-looking karat stamp on an earring post is an excellent indication of its gold content. It's not worth it for counterfeiters to buy the equipment needed to produce the tiny stamp on a post. They can make more money producing, for example, a fake 18K gold Italian necklace.

**Trademark Test**  Look for a manufacturer's mark along with the karat stamp. This is added assurance that the gold content is as stamped. Keep in mind, though, that existing trademarks can be counterfeited and fake ones can be created. So even if the jewelry has a trademark, it should still be tested, especially if you are not familiar with the trademark and the type of jewelry that manufacturer produces.

**Fig. 8.2** European mark for 14K--585.

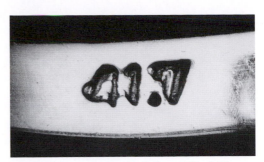

**Fig. 8.3** European mark for 10K--417

**Fig. 8.4** A poorly stamped 18K piece--750

**Fig. 8.5** KP means plumb gold, not plated gold.

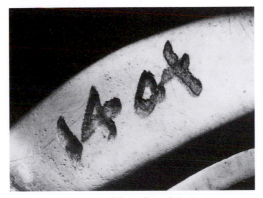

**Fig. 8.6** "Karat" abbreviated "ct" on an Australian piece.

**Fig. 8.7** Mark for 12K gold filled

**Color Test**

Note the color of the jewelry. It should look like gold, not copper or brass. Check if the color is evenly distributed. If it isn't, gold plating may have worn off the base metal or the piece might be part gold and part another metal. For example, the back of a necklace may be 18k gold and stamped as such, whereas the front, which is less likely to be tested, may be 10K.

Check around the hinges or clasps for color differences and signs of wear. This is an indication of plating (fig. 8.8). This can be verified by filing the piece in an inconspicuous spot and comparing the color underneath to the color on the surface.

**Fig. 8.8** Note the dark areas where plating has worn away

**Closed Back Test**

If the jewelry contains gemstones, look at the back of the setting. Is the bottom of the stone(s) blocked from view or enclosed in metal? (fig. 8.9) Do the stones look like they have been glued in rather than set? (fig. 8.10) Fake stones are commonly set or glued in fake-gold mountings. Genuine gems usually have open-back settings.

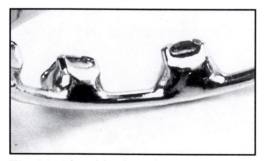

**Fig. 8.9** Closed-back setting

**Fig. 8.10** Fake stones glued in mounting

**Price Test**  If the jewelry is for sale, is it being sold at an unbelievably low price? If so, it's likely to be plated or underkarated. Even jewelers use price as a warning sign of low-karat or plated gold. They know there's no point in selling gold below cost or without making a profit. When a deal seems too good to be true, it probably is.

## Acid Testing for the Layperson

Standard acid tests for gold are based on the fact that gold will not react to pure nitric acid ($HNO_3$) but it will react to **agua regia,** a mixture of nitric and hydrochloric acid (HCl). These acid tests are usually more reliable than the above tests.

Acid testing is relatively inexpensive. You can separate imitation gold from 14K yellow gold and above with the aid of just one bottle of 14K gold testing liquid. (At a jewelry supply store or rock shop, it will normally range from $3 to $5. An acid-resistant plastic bottle is better than the glass type because it's non-breakable, air-tight, and spill-proof.) For safety reasons you should also have some baking soda, rubber gloves (the kitchen type will do), and safety glasses (these cost as little as $2 in jewelry supply, hardware, and chemical supply stores).

After you have the above supplies, as well as a jar of water and some white paper towels, follow the steps below. It's advisable to first practice on known metals.

♦ Take your jewelry and testing supplies to a well-ventilated area (e.g., outdoors, in a large garage, or on a patio).

♦ With the rubber gloves and safety glasses on, place a small drop of acid on an inconspicuous spot of the piece you want to test. If the drop bubbles and hisses, the piece is definitely fake gold. (If the piece you're testing is 10K gold or less, the acid drop will probably leave a brown stain. To avoid staining the piece, use the touchstone test described in the next chapter.}

♦ Observe if the drop changes color. The list of metals below with their color reaction to nitric acid will help you interpret the results.

| | |
|---|---|
| 18K gold + | no change |
| 14K gold | no change or a slight browning |
| 10K gold | turns brown |
| low karat gold | turns brown and green |
| platinum | no change |
| silver | turns white or gray |
| stainless steel | usually no change |
| copper, nickel | turn green |
| brass | turns green |

If you question the color change, also blot the piece with the white paper towel and look at the stain. A green and/or brown color is sometimes more evident as a stain. Keep a mental note of the color of the stain of various metal types. This is also a means of identifying metals.

Note that white metals other than white gold may show no reaction to the acid. The heaviness of platinum and lightness of stainless steel are helpful in separating these metals from white gold. Jewelry supply stores also sell a platinum testing acid.

Yellow gold is the only yellow metal which shows no reaction to nitric acid. (However, 10K gold turns brown due to the high percentage of alloy metals.) No color change or bubbling means either that the yellow piece is gold or gold plated. Continue with the next steps.

♦ If the drop of acid shows no reaction, file the piece in an inconspicuous spot. Look at the spot with a hand magnifier and compare the color of the metal surface to that of the filed area. If they are different, the piece is probably plated. Yellow **vermeil**, sterling silver plated or layered with gold, is easily detected by this method (color photo 9a). (**Sterling silver** is 92.5% silver and 7.5% copper. Its fineness mark is **925**.)

Karat gold is sometimes plated to give it a stronger yellow color. For example, a lot of 14K Italian chains are plated with 18K gold. Therefore, color differences are not always an indication of imitation gold.

**Fig. 8.11** Gold testing supplies

♦ After the piece is filed, place a drop of acid in the notch. Look for bubbling and for green, brown, white or gray colors. If you see none, look at the piece close up through a hand magnifier with your safety glasses on. (The fumes from the acid can damage your eyes.) White gold plating on sterling is one of the hardest imitations to detect and often magnification is required to see its reaction to the acid.

Gold buyers report that the plating on jewelry is getting thicker, particularly on the areas where the piece is most likely to be tested (e.g., on clasps, between links and on the inside of bracelets). Even jewelers have been fooled by some of the plated bangle bracelets and heavy link chain that are currently being sold. Filing is a necessity, when testing gold.

♦ After testing with acid, dip the piece in a jar of water mixed with a couple of spoonfuls of baking soda. This will stop the acid reaction on the alloy of the metal. Then rinse the piece with water. If acid gets on your rubber gloves, you can dip them in the jar and rinse with water. The acid must be neutralized, not merely diluted, especially if it gets on your skin.

♦ Put any paper towels used for blotting or wiping acid in a ziploc plastic bag. Add some baking powder to the bag. If the towels have more than a few tiny droplets of acid on them, baking soda may not be enough to neutralize the acid. See the section on acid disposal for proper disposal of hazardous wastes.

## Acid Testing for Jewelry Trade Professionals

The acid testing procedures above also apply to professionals, such as jewelers, appraisers, pawnbrokers, etc. However, greater precision is needed and legal requirements can differ.

In some communities it is illegal for businesses to buy or own any amount of acid without first obtaining a permit. (This includes the small bottles of gold testing liquid sold at jewelry supply stores. Households and hobbyists, however, are normally exempt from this regulation.) According to a Pasadena, California fire department official, businesses with small amounts of acid are often the least likely to know the proper precautions for using and disposing of acids. Plus, small amounts of acids in lots of bottles can add up to large amounts. Consequently, Pasadena requires businesses to have a permit in order to buy or use any amount of acid. Some other communities require permits only for large quantities of acid. Before buying or using acids, check with your local city government and/or fire department to find out what the regulations in your area are.

Jewelry-trade professionals are better off using pure acids rather than the premixed acids sold in jewelry stores. Some reasons for this are:

♦ Mixed acids tend to decompose faster than single acids. Gold testing liquids sold in the United States normally contain varying amounts of both nitric and hydrochloric acid (HCl), also called **muriatic acid**. Even the 10K liquid has a little HCl in it, even though jewelers typically test 10K gold only with nitric acid.

♦ The strength of the premixed acids may vary from one batch or supplier to another. For consistent results, the same strength and type of acid should always be used for a specific test. You can control this better, if you buy the individual acids yourself.

♦ It's easier to tell when pure acids are fresh because they fume more than the premixed gold testing liquids. A lack of fumes indicates the acid has lost its original strength. Stale acid can make 10K gold appear to be 14K.

♦ Pure acids are stronger than the ready-mixed acids. Consequently they may show clearer reactions. For example, the darker gray color reaction of pure nitric acid on silver is easier to see than the lighter gray produced by a 14K premixed solution.

Pure acids can be bought at chemical supply stores. They don't need to be diluted with water for gold testing. In fact the stronger they are, the more obvious the results. (Nitric acid from most chemical supply houses in Southern California is about 70% strength and HCl about 30%). Instead of using 14K gold testing liquid, professionals need only apply a drop of straight nitric acid to the unknown filed metal to determine if it is gold. HCl is needed to determine the fineness of high-carat gold. The next chapter explains that test.

Since the bottles from chemical supply stores contain more and stronger acid (4 oz may be the minimum size), greater precautions are needed when handling them. If you're not accustomed to pouring acids from one bottle into smaller bottles for testing, either have an experienced person do this for you or ask the chemical supply house to explain how. They will probably recommend stronger rubber gloves and a plastic apron. The small acid-resistant plastic bottles convenient for gold testing might not be sold at the chemical store. Jewelry supply stores often have them. When acids are exposed to air a lot, they get stale faster. Therefore, it's best to use the smaller bottles for gold testing and add fresh acid when needed.

Be careful where you store the acids. Besides being highly toxic, their fumes can damage your computers, appliances, and anything else you have that contains copper, nickel, brass, or silver. Naturally, make certain children can't reach them.

# Disposing of Acids

Regulations and arrangements for disposing of hazardous wastes vary from one town to another. Some cities may have a place where you can drop off your bottles of old acid at any time free of charge. Other cities may arrange a drop-off point at intervals such as once a month or twice a year. Depending on the type and quantity of acid, city officials may tell you how to neutralize it. A stronger substance than household baking soda is usually required.

To find out your city's disposal arrangements, call the fire department, city hall, or Board of Public Works. They can direct you to the department in charge. Cities often provide households with a free means of hazardous waste disposal.

Businesses may have to pay for acid disposal if it is not included in the price of their permit or license to use acids. Local regulations should be checked.

If you need to quickly dispose of some gold-testing acid but your city's disposal services are inconvenient, ask your jeweler if they or someone they know can take it from you. Some will accept it, just as some full-service gas stations will take old motor oil.

Never dispose of acids in garbage cans. Pets, children, and food scavengers can be permanently damaged if they come in contact with the acid while rummaging through the trash.

## Safety Tips for Using Acids

This chapter has already indicated precautions for acid testing. It helps, however, to have them summarized.

◆ Use acids only in a well-ventilated area. Don't breathe in the fumes.

◆ Wear rubber gloves.

◆ Wear safety glasses, especially when opening or pouring acids and when looking at acid reactions with hand magnifiers.

◆ Open acid bottles away from your face. The fumes may rush to your face.

◆ Never pour water into acid. This makes acid spit. To mix the two liquids, pour acid gradually into water.

◆ Keep baking soda nearby to neutralize acid.

◆ Do not let acid flow onto gemstones. Acid will etch or discolor many gems.

◆ Keep acid bottles tightly closed. Sometimes the acid eats away at the lids, and they need to be replaced to prevent the fumes from escaping.

◆ Store acid in a safe place away from children. Avoid extremes of temperature.

# Chapter 8 Quiz

1. Which of the following can help you distinguish between karat gold and gold-plated brass?
   a. a magnet
   b. nitric acid
   c. a trademark
   d. all of the above

2. A drop of nitric acid on a white metal shows no reaction. The metal could be:
   a. white gold
   b. platinum
   c. stainless steel
   d. any of the above
   e. none of the above

3. Acids should always be:
   a. stored in glass containers.
   b. diluted with distilled water
   c. kept away from children
   d. all of the above

## True or false?

4. 9K gold is a lot heavier than silver.

5. When doing acid tests, you should be in a well-ventilated area and have water and baking soda nearby.

6. Diamonds, rubies, and emeralds of high quality are often placed in closed-back settings to prevent them from being damaged.

7. If you accidently spill acid, wipe it up immediately and then throw away the cloth or paper towels in the trash bin.

## Answers:

1. b  Neither gold nor brass are magnetic. A trademark doesn't indicate gold quality.
2. d
3. c  A lot of jewelers and gold dealers prefer acid-resistant plastic bottles because they don't spill or break. In addition, plastic bottles are usually more air-tight than the glass type, so the acids last longer. Concentrated acids often provide more obvious test results than diluted acids.
4. F  Due to the high percentage of base metals, 9K gold is only slightly heavier than silver. The specific gravity of karat gold decreases as its purity goes down.
5. T
6. F  Closed-back settings are generally reserved for stones that are fake, assembled, or of very low quality.
7. F  You should first neutralize the acid with a substance such as bicarbonate of soda. Then wipe it up. Unneutralized acids or acid wipes should never be thrown in the trash bin. See section on acid disposal.

# 9

# Determining Karat Value (Fineness)

**T**he purity of gold is described by its **fineness**, parts per 1000, or by the **karat**, a 1/24 part of pure gold by weight. (The spelling "carat" is used in the British Commonwealth). Pure gold, is **alloyed** (mixed) with other metals to make it more durable and affordable or to change its color. The table below lists karat qualities of gold jewelry.

**Table 9.1:  Gold Content and Notation**

| Karats (USA) | Parts Gold | Gold % | Fineness (Europe) |
|---|---|---|---|
| 24K | 24/24 | 99.9% | 999 |
| 22K | 22/24 | 91.6% | 917 or 916 |
| 21K | 21/24 | 87.5% | 875 |
| 18K | 18/24 | 75.0% | 750 |
| 15K | 15/24 | 62.5% | 625 |
| 14K | 14/24 | 58.3% | 585 or 583 |
| 12K | 12/24 | 50.0% | 500 |
| 10K | 10/24 | 41.6% | 417 or 416 |
| 9K | 9/24 | 37.5% | 375 |
| 8K | 8/24 | 33.3% | 333 |

In France and Italy, gold must be at least 18K to be called gold.  In the US and Japan, the legal standard is 10K, in Spain, Britain, and Japan--9K, and in Germany--8K.  The two most common qualities of gold are 14K and 18K with 18K being the international standard for higher quality jewelry.

The previous chapter explained how to test for 10K and 14K gold.  The touchstone test described in the next section will help you test for 18K gold as well as other karat values.

## Touchstone Test

To do this test, you'll need a touchstone (a hard, fine-textured black stone sold in jewelry supply stores and some rock shops) and gold of known karat value. Gold test needles, which are marked according to the karat value of their gold tips, are typically used as a comparison reference. To test for 14K and below, nitric acid (or 14K fluid) is required. To test for 18K gold, you'll also need some hydrochloric acid (HCl) or some 18K gold testing liquid. Follow the procedure below using the same safety precautions outlined in the preceding chapter:

**Fig. 9.1** Materials for the touchstone test

♦ Make a wide line on the touchstone by rubbing the unknown metal back and forth. Rub hard to reach the possible base metal. Filing may be necessary to detect thick platings.

♦ Choose the needle that you think might have the same gold content as the unknown metal. With the needle, make a line of the same width and intensity either beside or above the unknown line. Compare their colors. Yellow gold usually has a deeper yellow color than metals that imitate it. (If you wish, make another line with a different test needle.)

♦ To test 14K gold, apply nitric acid or 14K liquid across the lines. Observe the color and check if they disappear. 14K gold should remain yellow and visible. Occasionally there may be a very slight browning. 10K gold can be compared to a streak from the 10K gold test needle. The acid may turn it brown, but sometimes the streak disappears before you see the brown color.

♦ To test 18K gold, use the opposite side of the touchstone. Add a drop of HCl after you apply the nitric acid to the known and unknown streaks. (The mixture of the these two acids is called **agua regia** and unlike nitric acid it will attack gold. A premixed 18K liquid from a jewelry supply store can also be used.) Note the rate and degree of disappearance. 18K gold should react like the 18K test needle streak.

Do not test 14K gold on the same touchstone surface as 18K. The residue left by the HCl can speed nitric acid reactions and make 14K gold appear to be 10K. It's a good idea to mark which side is for testing 18K gold and above.

♦ If the reaction is too fast for easy comparison, agua regia diluted with distilled water can be used. (But remember to pour acids into water, not vice versa, and do it slowly.) (Nitric acid diluted with distilled water is used by some people to test 10K gold. As with the diluted agua regia, the reaction on the touchstone will be slower and probably easier to compare to 8K and 12K.)

Michael Elliott of North American Metals in Van Nuys, California has found an easier method. He just rubs a little baby oil on the touchstone. This slows the reaction of the nitric acid and HCl droplet mixture.

♦ If you only have nitric acid, you can still make agua regia. Pour a bit of nitric acid in a separate bottle and add a pinch of common salt or a drop of a salt and distilled water solution (Gerald Wykoff, *Beyond the Glitter*, p. 85 and Kenneth Blakemore, *The Retail Jeweller's Guide*, p. 396).

A variety of agua regia formulas are used by jewelers. It probably doesn't matter which formula you use. What's important is that you use the same one consistently. The speed of the reaction is one of the main criteria for evaluating gold fineness and this will vary according to the strength and combination of the acids used. This book has only presented the easiest formulas in use.

♦ In summary, use concentrated nitric acid to test 14K gold and below. To test gold over 14K, turn the touchstone over. Place a drop of nitric acid on the streak. Add a drop of HCl. Note the color and speed of the reaction. Try to match them to a known streak.

When testing rings, test both the top and bottom of the ring. It's not uncommon for the shank to be of a different fineness. It's also a good idea to test both the front and back of necklaces.

At first, practice the touchstone test on jewelry you know. The more you do the touchstone test, the more accurate your results from it will be.

## Electronic Gold Testers

Portable electronic testers that measure the karat value of gold are available at jewelry supply stores (fig. 9.2). When the tip of the tester is applied to a metal, a digital reading will appear saying, for example, "18K" or "not gold." These testers range in cost from about $100 to $600. The cheaper ones are limited in the type of gold they can test and may only be able to indicate a special code for the gold content, instead of the karat value.

Some jewelers feel that gold testers are one of the best devices ever invented for the trade. Others say they are a waste of money. One written source states that although gold testers are accurate within 2 karats, they don't detect plating and gold overlay, and they leave a mark on items that are 14K and below, especially on white gold.

**Fig. 9.2** Electronic gold tester. Photo courtesy Tri Electronics.

Gold testers can work if the user understands the principles of gold testing. No matter what gold testing method is used, the base metal below gold plating or overlay must be tested in order for it to be detected. Proper filing will allow the base metal to be reached, even with a pin prick of the gold tester. If a piece is plated, the digital reading will decrease the deeper the piece is filed and tested. Solid karat gold will continue to give the same reading. Some of the less expensive testers may not be able to test the filed area.

The mark left on jewelry by gold testers can be polished away. It should be noted that a drop of nitric acid on 14K gold and below can also leave a mark. On a 10K piece, the stain from the drop can be more noticeable than the mark left by a gold tester.

Before testing an unknown material with a gold tester, you should try it on some metal you know. Just as acids can go bad, so can the solution or gel used by the gold tester.

Even though gold testers are not an essential tool for jewelers, they do provide a quick, convenient means of checking gold fineness. The people that get the best results from these testers are those who use it along with other tests.

## Two Gold Testing Examples

Concrete examples allow for a better understanding of the principles of gold testing. The first example for this section is a braided herringbone bracelet (fig 9.3). It feels lightweight, it's trademarked, and it has a fineness mark of 925. The fineness table at the beginning of this chapter does not list 925.

The number could be a stock number, but it happens to be the fineness mark for sterling silver. When the piece is filed and viewed through a hand magnifier, the silver color underneath is easy to see. Nitric acid turns the metal underneath a dull gray, so it is in fact silver (color photo 9a). If the bracelet is just rubbed lightly onto a touchstone, it tests as 18K gold.

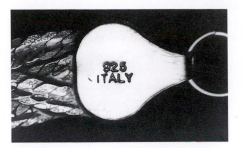

**Fig. 9.3** Gold-plated braided herring-bone with the sterling silver mark--925

This bracelet is sterling silver with a layer of mechanically bonded 18K gold. This may sound like a very valuable piece, but it's retail cost was $9.75. That's what it's worth. This first gold-testing example is an easy one, the next one isn't.

A neighbor brought the author a hollow gold bead necklace marked 14K (color photo 9c). It had been passed down in her family and she wondered if it really was 14K. Since the beads were hollow the weight was misleading. The necklace had the following characteristics.

♦ It was not magnetic. If it had been, this would have indicated a core of iron or stainless steel.

♦ There was no trademark.

♦ The color and surface texture looked fake, especially under magnification.

♦ The area between the beads was a different color than the outer part--light yellow with occasional black spots as opposed to deep yellow.

♦ When filed, the metal underneath showed a different lighter yellow color.

♦ The string holding the beads had a slight greenish tint.

♦ The reaction to the touchstone test varied from 14K to 18K depending on how hard the pieced was rubbed onto the stone.

The author was afraid to put acid on the piece for fear of it flowing onto the string. Since the test results were questionable, the necklace was taken to a gold assayer. Using the acid drop and touchstone test, he determined the necklace and clasp to be 14K gold.

To be absolutely certain that the necklace was 14K throughout, one would have to cut through a bead and test the inner part with acid, but there was no point in doing that in this case. There's also a possibility that some beads are gold and some aren't.

Color differences between the outer surface and inner part of a gold piece do not necessarily indicate it is fake. 14K Italian gold chains are commonly plated with 18K to give them a deeper yellow color. 14K jewelry may even be plated with 24K gold.

The main thing we should learn from this example, is that gold testing is not always clear-cut. Some pieces are easy to test, others may require professional assistance. But even experts admit that in some cases they have to cut completely through a piece to really know what's underneath the surface. Testing white metals, in particular, can be tricky.

To get an exact determination of gold content, a **fire assay** test must be done. A small sample of the gold in question is weighed and melted. Then by processes of oxidation, absorption, and dissolving in acid, the metals of the alloy are separated. The weight of the pure gold that results is compared to the original weight of the gold sample, and the fineness is calculated.

Fire assays are lengthy, expensive and destructive. So despite their accuracy, they aren't practical for general jewelry appraisal. As a consequence, the touchstone and acid-drop methods still remain the most popular tests for gold.

# Why Gold Tests Sometimes Fail

Gold testing must be done properly to be reasonably accurate. Even a gold assay can give false results if done wrong. When doing the acid tests described in this book, you should allow for a tolerance of about plus or minus two karats. However, if a metal is misidentified or the karat-value test results are off by 4 or more karats, this is probably due to one or more of the following reasons:

1.  The metal being tested was not filed. This is essential for the detection of heavy plating and overlay.

2.  The acid is old and stale. Weak acid can make 10K gold test like 14K. Check acids and electronic gold testers with known samples before using them to test unknowns.

3.  The acid is contaminated. Do not let the acid or bottle tip come in contact with metal, the touchstone, or other acid.

4.  The test needles are corroded from acid fumes and therefore give false results. Do not store them next to acids.

5.  The same side of the touchstone was used to test both high and low karat gold. The residue left by agua regia or 18K liquid during touchstone testing can make 14K gold test like 10K. Reserve a different side or stone for each test fluid used.

6. The width and intensity of the comparison streaks are different. A lightly rubbed streak can appear to be of a lower karat value than if it's rubbed hard on the touchstone (color photo 9e).

7. A magnifier was not used to view the test reaction. Sometimes acid reactions are not visible to the naked eye, especially on white-gold plated silver.

8. Only one section of a piece was tested. Both the head and shank of rings should be tested. Necklaces and bracelets should be tested both on the clasp and at least one place in between. Keep in mind too, that a solder joint may test lower than the rest of the piece.

9. The tester was influenced by a karat marking or by what he or she wanted to see. Preconceptions can keep us from being objective and from doing the required number of tests. One advantage of the electronic gold tester is that if it says 14K, it's hard to read 18K. It's easier to misread the reaction of a streak on a touchstone.

10. Only one test was done. Gold experts often find it necessary to do both the touchstone test and the acid drop test. Weight, color, markings, and magnetic attraction must also be considered when determining the identity of a metal. Gemologists rely on a combination of tests to identify gems. People testing metals should do the same.

## Subtle Deception Techniques

There are legal ways to mislead buyers. For example, one gold dealer reports that in his town, merchants who had been convicted of selling 10K gold stamped 14K, discovered they could sell just as much 10K gold by stamping it **417**, the European fineness mark for 10K. Uninformed American buyers either think it's "14" written backwards or else a stock number. In most cases, they don't even bother to look at the stamp or ask what karat gold they are buying. The only thing that matters is the price tag. American-made 14K gold, however, is usually stamped 14K not 585.

Some sellers like to take advantage of the fact that gold prices can be based on grams or pennyweights (1 g = 0.643 penneyweight). They may sell by the gram and buy by the pennyweight. When getting price quotes by weight, be sure you understand the unit of weight used.

Hollow gold jewelry and chains offer consumers a big look at a low price. They offer some sellers a convenient means of deceiving their customers. A hollow chain that looks double its weight may seem to be a bargain compared to a solid one.

It is not uncommon to see yellow gold-plated sterling stamped **925**. There are probably some sellers hoping it will be interpreted as a high purity of gold. When you see 925, think silver not gold.

Don't assume that all the jewelry in a 14K display case is 14K gold. 10K pieces may also be mixed in (and so may some 18K). Therefore, it's best to verify with the salesperson the karat value of the jewelry you plan to buy.

In addition to displaying 10K and 14K gold together, stores may also place jewelry with synthetic (lab-grown or created) stones next to pieces with natural stones. There may be no signs saying lab-grown, and the salesperson may forget to mention they're synthetic. The main reason for displaying lab-grown stones with natural ones is to make them appear as valuable as natural ones when in fact they aren't. Limited space is occasionally a factor too. Do not assume that all the gems you see in a jewelry case are natural.

To avoid being misled, buyers need to be informed. They should ask the following questions and have the answers written on their purchase receipt.

♦ What karatage gold is it?

♦ Is the gold solid or hollow?

♦ Are the gemstones natural or lab-grown (synthetic)?

A reputable jeweler will include this information on sales receipts and appraisal reports regardless of whether you ask or not. He/she wants you to know even more than this about your jewelry because as one Chicago jeweler states, "An informed consumer is the Industry's best advertisement for expanded business. The more you know, the more you will feel confident in buying and the more you will appreciate the art and beauty of jewelry."

## Which is better, 14K or 18K?

18K (750) gold has 3/4 gold and 1/4 other material whereas 14K (585) is just a little more than half gold. This means that 18K gold is more valuable. It's also less likely to cause a reaction in people who are allergic to metals alloyed with gold, and it usually has a deeper yellow color than 14K gold.

The author, in her book, *The Diamond Ring Buying Guide*, mentions that 14K gold has the advantage of wearing better than 18K gold. A German jeweler, upon reading this, said,

> "That's utter nonsense. Europeans wear 18K jewelry all the time and they
> don't have any problems with it. Have a look at my wedding ring. It's 22
> karats. It's been worn for years and is almost like new."

There are many other jewelers who believe that 14K is, in fact, more durable than 18K gold. The best way of resolving the question is to compare the hardness (resistance to scratching) and tensile strength (resistance to fracture) of some 14 and 18K gold alloys. The table below provides this data for pure gold and eight of its alloys.

## Table 9.2

| Gold Type | % Composition | | | | | | Hardness | | T Strength |
|---|---|---|---|---|---|---|---|---|---|
| | Au | Ag | Cu | Zn | Ni | Pd | Annealed[1] | Cold Worked[2] | (daN/mm2)[3] |
| Pure gold | 99.9 | | | | | | 20 HV[4] | 50 HV | 28 |
| 14K yellow | 58.5 | 20.5 | 21 | | | | 190 HV | 260 HV | 58 |
| 14K white | 58.5 | | 25.8 | 0.4 | 15.3 | | 177 HB[5] | | 70 |
| 14K white | 59 | | 26.0 | 8.0 | 7.0 | | 137 HV | 308 HV | 51 |
| 14K white | 59 | 28.5 | 1.5 | 0.1 | 0.9 | 10 | 82 HV | 195 HV | 41 |
| 18K yellow | 75 | 12.5 | 12.5 | | | | 150 HV | 225 HV | 51 |
| 18K white | 75 | | 11.0 | 14.0 | 14.0 | | 220 HV | 350 HV | 71 |
| 18K white | 75 | 10.5 | 3.5 | 0.1 | 0.9 | 10 | 95 HV | 216 HV | 38 |

Data based on Tables A-1 and A-2 of *Professional Goldsmithing* by Alan Revere (p. 206), which were adapted from Grimwade (1985) and Alloy Data Sheets supplied by the World Gold Council (1990).

Au = gold, Ag = silver, Cu = copper, Zn = zinc, Ni = nickel, Pd = Palladium.

1. **Annealed** metal has been heated to its specific annealing temperature and then immersed rapidly in water. This causes the metal grains to recrystallize into larger sizes, restoring the metal's workability. The annealing temperatures of the above alloys are indicated on page 206 of *Professional Goldsmithing*.

2. **Cold worked** refers to the bending, twisting, and rolling processes, which compress the grains of the metal, making it harder.

3. 1 daN = 1.02 kg force. The tensile strength data in this table refers to the maximum load that can be applied to annealed metal without reducing its diameter or breaking it. The higher the number the stronger the metal.

4. & 5. HV = Hardness Vickers, HB = Hardness Brinell. These are metal hardness measuring systems. Brinell and Vickers values below 300 are very close. The higher the number the harder the metal.

Some of the conclusions that can be drawn when analyzing the above data are:

♦ Yellow 14K gold is harder and stronger than yellow 18K gold.

♦ Nickel white gold is harder than palladium white gold.

♦ Most important, it's not the color or gold content of an alloy which determines its hardness and strength. The metals alloyed with the gold and their proportions are what mainly control gold durability. (Other factors can also play a role--e.g., mode of fabrication and whether it's freshly refined or old gold.)

Whether a piece of jewelry is 14K or 18K is usually not an important issue.  What matters most is whether you can find a jewelry piece you like in your price range.  In North America, you'll have a better selection of 14K jewelry because a greater variety of it is manufactured, although 18K is making stronger than ever gains in sales.  Much of the better jewelry is still made in 18K, even in the US.  In Europe, due to tradition and sometimes government regulations, 18K is often more readily available.  In India and Southeast Asia, 22K gold is popular because people there regard it as a monetary investment and like its deep yellow color.

If you are having a piece custom made, you can usually choose the percentage of the gold. Consider what you can afford and whether you have ever had allergic reactions to karat gold. Explain to the jeweler how often and where you plan to wear the piece and describe your color preferences.  Together, you'll be able to determine the gold that best fits your needs and your pocketbook.

# Chapter 9 Quiz

1. What are the European fineness marks for 10K, 14K, 18K and 22K gold?

2. A $500 electronic gold tester accurately tests 6 samples of 10, 14, and 18K gold, but fails to detect a plated sample. This is probably because:

   a. The gold tester is defective.
   b. Electronic gold testers can't detect plated gold.
   c. The plated sample was not filed to allow the base metal to be tested.

3. A drop of nitric acid on a white metal turns it grey. This means the metal is probably:

   a. white gold          c. stainless steel
   b. silver              d. nickel

## True or False?

4. If a drop of nitric acid turns a yellow metal brown, then the metal is not karat gold.

5. If a yellow-metal necklace is stamped 925 and has a trademark, it is probably made of a very high karat gold.

6. For an exact determination of gold content, a fire assay test is required.

7. All 14K white gold has the same hardness and strength.

8. If an unknown metal reacts as 14K gold to the touchstone test, it may in fact be 12 or 13K.

9. One reason why people misidentify metals is that they rely only on one test.

## Answers:

1. 10K = 416 or 417, 14K = 583 or 585, 18K = 750, 22K = 916 or 917.
2. c
3. b
4. F  Nitric acid usually turns 10K gold brown.
5. F  It's probably sterling silver plated or bonded with gold.
6. T
7. F  The hardness and strength of gold varies depending on the metals it is alloyed with.
8. T  When doing the touchstone test, you should allow for a tolerance of about ±2 karats.
9. T

# 10

# Gold Colors

**W**hat color is gold? It's not yellow. To prove this, find an object that looks pure bright yellow and compare it to a piece of gold jewelry. The colors will be different.

Because of gold's metallic luster and the way in which it reflects the surroundings, it's not easy to determine its color. However, when you analyze it carefully, you discover that the color of gold is a combination of light brown, yellow and orange. Nevertheless, gold is referred to as a yellow metal.

If you have ever compared a 14K Italian-made chain to one made in the USA, you've probably noted that the American-made one has a lighter color (color photo 10a). This is normally because it contains more silver and less copper than the one made in Italy. Sometimes, too, Italian 14K chains are plated with 18K or 24K gold to produce this effect. Europeans prefer a deeper gold color and so do Asians. (Plating is also used to make the color more uniform.)

Even within Europe, yellow gold will vary in color. As a consequence, it may be hard to match gold mountings and their components (clasps, settings, etc.). To alleviate this problem, gold sample plates for standard alloys are used there.

The Manufacturing Jewelers and Silversmiths of America (MJSA) is trying to develop a color reference system too. This would allow American jewelers to order gold alloys by a code name such as 14KY1 or 14KY2 so they could more easily match gold colors. The MJSA is in contact with European organizations and hopes that some day (perhaps in the next century) there may be an international gold color reference system.

Gold alloys not only come in varying shades of yellow, they may also be green, pink, or white. The pinker the alloy, the more copper it contains. The greener it is, the more silver it has.

There are various white gold alloys but the most common ones contain gold, nickel, copper, and zinc. Most of these white gold alloys were developed after World War II as a substitute for platinum. Prior to the war, platinum was the preferred choice for diamond rings in America, but when the US government declared platinum a strategic metal, it was no longer available for jewelry use. By the early 60's, yellow gold had become the preferred metal for diamond rings, and white gold tended to be associated with silver, not platinum. This trend is reversing now that platinum is becoming increasingly popular.

Gold alloys that look red, blue, black or purple do exist, but they are seldom made into jewelry because they are very difficult or impossible to work with. Curiously, when purple gold is formed by melting gold and aluminum together, the resulting compound loses some of its metallic properties.

A table indicating the composition of different gold alloys is presented below. It will give you a better understanding of how colored gold is formed. The table is mostly based on an article entitled "A Jeweler's Guide to Gold in Technicolor" by Tom Arnold from the December 1984 issue of *The Goldsmith*. Other formulas are also used to create the various gold colors.

## Table 10.1   Some 18K Gold Alloys and Their Colors

|  | % gold | silver | copper | aluminum | iron | cadmium |
|---|---|---|---|---|---|---|
| yellow | 75 | 9.5 | 15.5 | | | |
| light yellow | 75 | 11.5 | 13.5 | | | |
| light green | 75 | | 23.0 | | | 2 |
| deep green | 75 | 25.0 | | | | |
| med. green | 75 | 5.0 | 20.0 | | | |
| bright red | 75 | | | 25 | | |
| blue | 75 | | | | 25 | |
| grey | 75 | | 8.0 | | 17 | |

| | % gold | silver | copper | zinc | nickel | palladium |
|---|---|---|---|---|---|---|
| pink | 75 | 5 | 20 | | | |
| med rose | 75 | 2.75 | 22.25 | | | |
| deep rose | 75 | | 25 | | | |
| brown | 75 | 6.25 | | | | 18.75 |
| white | 75 | | | | | 25 |
| white | 75 | | | 11 | 14 | |

Occasionally surface techniques are used to color karat gold. In the chapters on gold testing, it was mentioned that nitric acid will turn 10K gold dark brown. Gold can also be darkened through oxidation when heated. Color photo 10b shows how a naturalistic coloring was achieved on a bird brooch by first oxidizing the 9K gold to a black color. Later the other colors were exposed using scraping techniques.

# Black HIlls Gold Jewelry

To some, Black Hills gold jewelry is just a souvenir to buy when visiting Mount Rushmore. Black Hills gold, however, is sold in jewelry stores throughout the United States. You'll find it in other countries too. Besides pendants and earrings, the Black Hills jewelry manufacturers, design wedding ring sets, bracelets, watches, belt buckles, money clips, coin bezels--in other words, all types of jewelry (figs. 10.1-3 and color photos 10f-h).

The distinguishing characteristics of Black Hills gold jewelry are as follows:

♦ It is made in the Black Hills area of South Dakota--the southwestern part of the state, which includes Rapid City, Deadwood, and Belle Fourche.

♦ It has a grape-leaf motif. Some of the more traditional pieces also have designs with grape clusters and tendrils.

♦ It has pink and green gold leaves soldered to a yellow gold mounting, giving it a tri-color look. A copper alloy is used to make the pink gold, and a silver alloy is used to make the pale green gold.

**10b** Lady's and man's watches. *Photo courtesy Stamper.*

**10a** Money clips. *Photo courtesy of Landstrom's.*

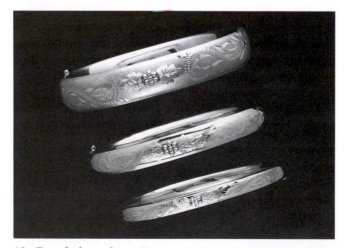

**10c** Bangle bracelets. *Photo courtesy South Dakota Gold.*

♦ The mountings are usually of 10K gold, the leaves of 12K. The mountings, however, can be special ordered in 14 and 18K gold. The 14K wedding sets are entirely of 14K gold, leaves included.

♦ The grape leaves are finished with a process called **wriggling**. A blade is passed back and forth across the leaf with a continuous, vibrating motion. This gives the leaves their textured, frosty appearance.

♦ Some of the gold in the jewelry may originate from the Homestake Mine in Lead, South Dakota.

Black Hills jewelry is a good example of how different manufacturing processes can be combined to create unique pieces. The mountings are cast, the grape leaves are die-struck (stamped), components called curls are hand fabricated from wire, the veins in the leaves are hand engraved by some Black Hills gold manufacturers.

As with any jewelry, the quality can vary depending on who makes it. Lower quality pieces can be porous, badly soldered, lack-luster and very lightweight. The better quality ones are sturdier and have a brighter finish, particularly on the leaves.

Black Hills gold is an original American art form. According to the Black Hills gold manufacturers, Indian jewelry is the only other category of jewelry that holds this honor. Black Hills gold jewelry might date back to 1876 when a French goldsmith, Henri LeBeau, opened a shop in Central CIty, South Dakota. Some say LeBeau got his inspiration for the grape-leaf motif through a dream about the beautiful vineyards of his homeland. A few say the wild grapes of South Dakota saved LeBeau's life after he became lost while searching for gold. Other stories exist as well.

What is fact is that the Black Hills region was the site of one of the world's major gold rushes. This rush resulted in the third largest gold mine in the United States, the Homestake (*Gold Minerals Yearbook 1989*, page 7). The mine is spread over 200 miles and still produces over 350,000 ounces of gold per year (*Man and His Gold*, a booklet produced by the Gold Information Center). Much of it is used for Black Hills jewelry. It's not the gold, though, that makes this jewelry so distinctive. It's the grape-leaf motif created by Black Hills craftsmen.

## Which is Better--A White Gold, Yellow Gold, or Platinum Setting?

When choosing the setting for an expensive stone such as a diamond, the question often arises as to what metal would hold the stone most securely. The answer depends on the alloy used. Compare the hardness, toughness, and density (heaviness and compactness) of the alloys in the following tables:

# TABLE 10.2 Properties of Platinum Alloys

| | Composition % | | | | Hardness | | Tensile Strength | Density |
|---|---|---|---|---|---|---|---|---|
| Plat. | Iridium | Pd | Ruthenium | Cobalt | Annealed[1] | Cold worked[2] | (daN/mm$^2$)[3] | (g/cm3) |
| 99.9 | | | | | 50HV | 108HV | 29-33 | 21.4 |
| 95 | 5 | | | | 80HV | 170HB | 58 | 21.4 |
| 95 | | | 5 | | 130HV | 211HB | 87 | 20.7 |
| 95 | | | | 5 | 135HV | | | 20.8 |
| 90 | 10 | | | | 110HV | 220HB | 80 | 21.5 |
| 90 | | 10 | | | 80HV | 160HB | | 19.8 |
| 85 | | 15 | | | 90HV | | | 19.1 |

Data based mainly on tables in "Platinum Jewelry Products" by Johnson Matthey and Tables XLIII and XLIV of *Working In Precious Metals* by Ernest Smith (pp. 300 & 301).

1    **Annealed** metal has been heated to its specific annealing temperature and then immersed rapidly in water.
2    **Cold worked** refers to the bending, twisting, and rolling processes, which compress the grains of the metal, making it harder.
3    1 daN = 1.02 kg force.  The higher the number, the greater the tensile strength (resistance to fracture).
4, 5  HV = Hardness Vickers, HB = Hardness Brinell.  These are metal hardness measuring systems.  Brinell and Vickers values below 300 are very close.  The higher the number the harder the metal.

The platinum/ruthenium and platinum/iridium alloys above are the ones most frequently used in jewelry.
Platinum/cobalt alloys are used for hard castings in Europe and Hong Kong.
The platinum/palladium alloys are mainly used in Hong Kong and Japan with the one of 85% platinum being used mainly for chain-making in Japan.

# TABLE 10.3 Properties of Gold Alloys

| Gold Type | % Composition | | | | | | Hardness | | T. Strength | Density |
|---|---|---|---|---|---|---|---|---|---|---|
| | Au | Ag | Cu | Zn | Ni | Pd | Annealed | Cold Worked | daN/mm$^2$ | g/cm$^3$ |
| Pure gold | 99.9 | | | | | | 20 HV[2] | 58 HV | 28 | 19.32 |
| 14K yellow | 58.5 | 20.5 | 21.0 | | | | 190 HV | 260 HV | 58 | 13.65 |
| 18K yellow | 75 | 12.5 | 12.5 | | | | 150 HV | 225 HV | 52 | 15.45 |
| 18K white | 75 | | 11.0 | | 14.0 | | 220 HV | 350 HV | 71 | 14.70 |
| 18K white | 75 | 10.5 | 3.5 | 0.1 | 0.9 | 10 | 95 HV | 216 HV | 38 | 16.08 |
| 17K white | 70 | | | | | 30 | 96 HB[3] | 124 HB | | |

Table 10-3 data based mainly on Tables A-1 and A-2 of *Professional Goldsmithing* by Alan Revere (p. 206), which were adapted from Grimwade (1985) and Alloy Data Sheets supplied by the World Gold Council (1990).

Au = gold, Ag = silver, Cu = copper, Zn = zinc, Ni = nickel, Pd = Palladium.

The data in the tables indicate that alloyed platinum is denser and usually stronger than most gold alloys. It is softer than nickel white gold and 14 or 18K yellow gold. The lower hardness of platinum is mainly due to its higher purity. Both gold and platinum are relatively soft in their pure form, with gold being the softest of the two. However, they become harder as certain alloying metals are added. A 95% gold alloy would be softer than one which is 95% platinum.

Platinum settings are often said to be more durable than those of gold, and they can be more delicate, yet secure. This is due to the greater density and strength of platinum.

Platinum jewelry should have platinum settings. It is unethical to repair or size platinum jewelry with white gold without first getting the customer's permission. This is occasionally done, however, because karat gold costs less and doesn't demand the same amount of skill and time.

It's appropriate for gold jewelry to have either gold or platinum settings. White gold heads are often used on yellow gold rings to provide a hard, secure setting. The white gold can also enhance colorless diamonds. The same effect can be achieved by plating yellow-gold prongs with rhodium, a hard, white, highly reflective metal of the platinum family. The plating can wear off, though, and may need to be redone later.

Yellow gold is an ideal setting for yellowish diamonds because it can mask their yellowish tints. If a diamond is so yellow that it can be classified as a fancy color, a white gold or platinum setting would be better. The white metal would emphasize the yellow of the diamond.

# 11

# Gold-Coin Jewelry

Jeannette needed money, so she decided to take her gold American-Eagle coin pendant to a coin dealer. She figured he would give her the going rate for the coin plus an additional amount for the **coin bezel** (pendant mounting for coins). Since the coin had been badly worn down and had no significant **numismatic value** (coin-related value as opposed to intrinsic metal value), the dealer said he could only offer her a scrap-gold rate for the whole pendant. In this case, it would be 90% of the **spot price of gold** (the current cash price at which the major gold exchanges are listing and selling their gold). He could never resell the scratched worn-down American Eagle for the same price as a brand new one. Jeannette was upset. The pendant she bought as an investment, was worth much less than she had paid for it. This was because gold prices had dropped; labor costs for making it could not be recouped; and the coin was not in saleable condition.

If Jeannette's main intention was to trade in the coin later on, she should not have bought it as a pendant. Mounting coins in jewelry can decrease their resale and numismatic value if the coins are damaged by wear or by the setting process. The value of coin jewelry may go up if the price of gold or the numismatic value increases. However, this cannot be guaranteed.

## Why Buy Coin Jewelry?

Gold-coin jewelry has been worn for centuries. In recent years, it has become increasingly popular because of the abundance of new governmental and commemorative coins. Some of the reasons for buying coin jewelry are as follows:

♦ **As a fashion accessory**. Gold coins are beautiful and they are different. No matter what style of clothing you're wearing--classic, dramatic, casual, or fancy--coin jewelry can provide an attractive accent.

♦ **As a way of displaying a work of art**. Gold coins are among the finest crafted coins in existence. Their high value justifies considerable artistic effort in the design of the coin, and the malleability of the gold allows them to be stamped with sharp, intricate engravings.

♦ **As a memento of your native country or a souvenir** of a country you have visited. You can get more enjoyment from the coin if you wear it than if you just store it in a box.

♦ **As a gift**. No matter what a person's tastes are, they will appreciate a gold coin. When the coin is set in jewelry, people are more likely to hold on to it and remember who gave it to them. Since there are a variety of sizes available, you should be able to find a gold coin that fits your budget.

♦ **As a collector's item**. Animal lovers, for example, may wish to collect and wear coins such as the Chinese Panda, the Singapore Tiger or Horse, the Gibraltar Dog (fig 11.1), and the endangered wildlife series of the Cook Islands. People with pet cats love the Cat coin from The Isle of Man (color photo 11b). They show it off in jewelry to their friends and tell them "That's my little kitty."

♦ **As a means of remembering a loved one** who has left the coin(s) as part of an inheritance. Both jewelers and coin dealers sell mountings for coins. If you can't find a mounting to fit your coin(s), one can always be custom made.

**Fig. 11.1** Gibraltar dog coin.
*Photo courtesy HH Gold.*

♦ **As a sentimental souvenir of a date, place, or event**. For example, gold coins with the year of a birth, anniversary, graduation, baptism, bar mitzvah, etc. make appropriate gifts. They also make ideal awards. Companies may give a long-time employee a coin with the year in which he or she started work, or they may award coins representing the countries in which they operate.

♦ **As a limited form of investment**. The premium charged for gold bullion coins is usually a lot less than the average retail markup on jewelry, and labor costs are not added to the price of coins. This means that although gold coins may lose their full metal value after mounting, in most cases, they retain more of it than regular jewelry.

In addition, buyers don't question the gold content of a gold bullion coin, such as the Canadian Maple Leaf. But a rope chain stamped 14K may be calculated at less than 14K if the dealer suspects it has been underkarated or contains a lot of low-karat solder. Gold buyers would rather underestimate the gold content than lose money on a piece that has less gold than marked.

When gold bullion coins are issued in limited quantities, they may also be valuable from a numismatic standpoint. For example, some of the original Chinese Panda one-ounce coins have sold for over $3000.

## Practical Considerations for Buying Coin Jewelry

When buying coin jewelry, it's important to consider how often and where it will be worn. If you plan to wear it every day both for work and dress, it needs to be more durable than if it's only worn occasionally. Keep the following points in mind:

♦ Pure gold is very soft and wears down easily. A 24K coin such as the Maple Leaf or Panda is best worn as a pendant, tie tac, or pin. For rings, bracelets, or cuff links, a 22K coin such as the American Eagle or Britannia is a more practical choice. Gold alloyed with other metals is harder and more resistant to wear than pure gold. But even most 22K alloys are relatively soft compared to 14 and 18K gold.

**Fig. 11.2** Ladies' coin rings. *Photo courtesy Wideband Jewelry.*

**Fig. 11.3** Man's coin ring. *Photo courtesy Hallock Coin Jewelry.*

♦ Ring mountings with the prongs underneath the coin rather than on top are less likely to get caught on clothing and fabric-covered furniture. However, coins that are prong set from the bottom can sometimes jar loose when hit. That's why it's important to choose a good quality ring mounting with secure prongs.

♦ Prong-set coin pendants are more likely to damage the coin than the screw-type, in which coins slide into a slot and are held in place by a screw or bolt. If pressed hard against the coin, prongs can leave a mark. If prongs are not secure, the coin can rotate in the bezel, and a circular line results.

The screw-top bezels may cost a little more, but they're easier to mount and normally do not damage the coin. They can also be worn from either side because there are no prongs on the backside. Coins can look equally attractive from the back and front.

Occasionally, the screw may come loose or back out of the bezel. This can be prevented by choosing a well-made mounting and by putting a dab of clear nail polish in the screw hole. The screw can be loosened afterwards by soaking it in acetone.

**Fig. 11.4** Screw-top coin bezel. *Photo courtesy Wideband Jewelry.*

♦ Coins should not be defaced. Do not drill a hole in a coin to suspend it on a chain. Some highly valued coins have been ruined in this way. There are plenty of coin mountings available in a wide variety of price ranges, making drilling unnecessary. Custom-made bezels can be designed for coins of irregular shapes or unusual sizes.

# Bullion Coins

Coins whose worth is based on the value of the metal they contain are called **bullion coins**. Originally, the word "bullion" meant "mint" or "melting place," and then it became a generic term for refined bars or ingots of gold or silver. (The English term "bullion" originates from the French "boullion" meaning something boiled like a soup broth.)

With the launching of the Krugerrand, South Africa introduced the concept of a one-ounce bullion coin without a declared face value. It was sold to large distributors at a premium of 3% over its gold content. Smaller 1/2, 1/4, and 1/10th troy-ounce coins were also produced.

The next bullion coin to be issued was the Canadian Maple Leaf, in 1979. On a worldwide basis, this is now the best selling bullion coin. Since then, several other bullion coins have been introduced. Some are listed in the table below, along with their gold fineness, country, and face value (if applicable).

One of the main reasons for the popularity of the Maple Leaf is that it is 24K gold, unlike the American Eagle (the US bullion coin) which is 22K. Many of the biggest buyers of gold are in the Orient, and they prefer pure, 24K-gold coins. The fact that the American Eagle is just 22K does not mean it has less gold than the Canadian Maple Leaf. Both one-ounce gold coins contain one ounce of gold, but the gross weight of the American Eagle is higher due to the additional alloying metals. In the table below, you'll find the gross weight of the various one-ounce gold-coins. Keep in mind that these coins are also produced in smaller sizes such as 1/2, 1/4. 1/10th and occasionally 1/20 or 1/25th of an ounce. The premium charged for the coins increases as their size decreases.

## One-ounce Bullion Coins

| Name | Country | Fineness | Gross Weight | Face Value |
|------|---------|----------|--------------|------------|
| Angel | Isle of Man | 917 | 1.09 oz t | |
| Britannia | Britain | 917 | 1.09 oz t | £100 |
| Cat (Crown) | Isle of Man | 999 | 1.00 oz t | |
| American Eagle | USA | 917 | 1.09 oz t | $50 |
| Krugerrand | South Africa | 917 | 1.09 oz t | |
| Maple Leaf | Canada | 999 | 1.00 oz t | $50 |
| Mexican Gold | Mexico | 900 | 1.11 oz t | |
| Nugget (Kangaroo) | Australia | 999 | 1.00 oz t | $100 |
| Panda | China | 999 | 1.00 oz t | 100 yuan |
| Philharmonic | Austria | 999 | 1.00 oz t | 2000 Schillings |
| Singapore (Lunar series) | | 999 | 1.00 oz t | $100 |

Some bullion coins, such as the American Eagle, the Britannia, and the Nugget are issued in special "proof" editions so they can be sold to collectors at higher premiums. These "proof" coins are struck two or more times with highly polished dies to enhance every detail.

The raised portions of their designs often have a frosted appearance whereas the rest of the coin's surface is typically as reflective as a mirror. Proof bullion coins were intended to be sold as collectibles, not for jewelry wear or circulation. However, they are sometimes set in jewelry, especially when their premiums are relatively low. Plastic inserts in screw-top bezels have been occasionally used to protect them.

Fig. 11.5 Angel coin from the Isle of Man. *Photo courtesy HH Gold.*

Fig. 11.6 Liberty-Head Double Eagle. *Photo courtesy of Wideband Jewelry.*

# Other Coins

## Non-bullion-type legal-tender coins

Not all gold Eagle coins are bullion coins. The first ones issued were just **legal-tender** coins, which means they were officially worth their face value. In 1795, the first legal-tender US gold coins were struck, the $10 Eagles known simply as **Eagles**. The Eagle had a fineness of .917 and a fine gold content of 0.515 troy ounces. They were minted until 1804. In 1838, the $10 Eagles were reissued with a fineness of .900 and a pure gold content of 0.48375 troy ounces.

Other denominations of Eagle coins were also issued--$20 gold pieces called **Double Eagles**, $5 gold pieces called **Half Eagles**, and $2.50 gold pieces called **Quarter Eagles**. Gold dollar coins were produced too.

**9a** Dark gray stains from nitric acid on a filed, gold-plated sterling silver chain.

**9b** The green and brown color of the excess solder indicate it is not 14 karat gold.

**9c** 14K gold beads with a lighter base color than the surface. See gold testing example in chapter 9.

**9d** 14K gold-testing fluid on a penny, a sterling silver charm, a 10K heart pendant, and 18K gold. The acid on the 18K gold remained clear. (The dark spots are just reflections.) Concentrated nitric acid added later to the silver charm created dark gray stains as in photo 9a.

**9e** Touchstone test. Left--a 10K streak reaction to 14K liquid. The right streak appears to be of a higher karat value than the center streak. In this case, it's because the streaks were not applied with equal intensity. Both streaks were made with the same 14K gold piece.

**10b** Note the natural looking coloring of the migrant fieldfare (thrush) of this 9K gold brooch. The orange, brown, and black colors were created by heating the gold till it turned black through oxidation. Later the craftsman artfully worked down the metal to expose the gradations of color. See chapter 14. *Photo courtesy of the designer, Alan Hodgkinson.*

**10c** Clay model used to make the cast brooch above. *Photo courtesy Alan Hodgkinson.*

**10d**  18K white and yellow gold pin representing a 0.99 ct diamond fish in a porthole.  *Photo courtesy Global Diamonds, Inc.*

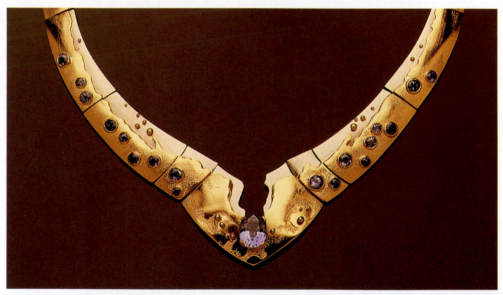

**10e**  18K white and yellow gold collar necklace set with Ceylon sapphires.  *Photo courtesy of Richard Kimball.*

**10f** Mothers' rings with the birthstones of their children. *Photo courtesy of South Dakota gold.*

**10g** Black Hills gold pendant with the traditional motif of grape leaves, grapes, and tendrils. *Photo courtesy of Landstrom's.*

**10h**  10K gold necklace and earrings accented with black onyx and pink and green 12K gold leaves. *Photo courtesy Stamper Black Hills Gold Jewelry.*

**10i**  Left: well-finished pair of leaves with good detail.  Compare their luster and frosted appearance to that of the quickly finished pair of leaves to the right.  Not all Black Hills gold jewelry is of the same quality. *Photo courtesy Stamper.*

**11a** Canadian Maple Leaf and American Eagle coin pendants. *Photo courtesy Wideband Jewelry.*

**11b** Isle of Man Cat and Chinese Panda coin pendants. *Photo courtesy Hallock Coin Jewelry.*

**11c** Singapore Dragon coin pendant.
*Photo courtesy HH Gold.*

**11d** Pearl enhancer. *Photo courtesy Wideband Jewelry.*

**11e** American Indian Head coin pendant.
*Photo courtesy HH Gold.*

**Fig. 11.7** Cuff links with Wilhelm II 20 Marks coins. *Photo courtesy Wideband Jewelry.*

**Fig. 11.8** Egyptian one-pound coin. *Photo courtesy Wideband Jewelry.*

**Fig. 11.9** A Mexican one-ounce gold piece and a 5 gram Credit Suisse ingot. *Photo courtesy Wideband Jewelry.*

Gold coins were minted until 1933, when the United States went off of the gold standard. In 1986, the US government started issuing gold bullion coins called **American Eagles**. These were intended to be an alternative to other popular world bullion coins such as the Canadian Maple Leaf.

A description of the legal-tender gold coins of the world, could fill a book. In fact there is a large book that's called *Gold Coins of the World*. Two coins that are particularly popular in the United States are the $2.50 Indian Head (for men's rings, due to its masculine look) and the smaller $1-Liberty Head (for women's rings). An example of a Liberty Head coin is given in figure 11.6--a Double Eagle (a $20 gold coin). Color photo 11e shows an Indian Head Eagle, (a $10 gold coin).

A good source of information for US gold coins is Yeoman's *A Guidebook of United States Coins*, referred to in the coin trade as "The Red Book." This is probably the best reference guide for US coins both in terms of its technical specifications and its coin pricing information (the prices given are based on the average retail price of the coins). A couple examples of coins from other countries are shown in figures 11.7-9.

## Commemorative gold coins

Commemorative coins are struck to honor important people, places, and historic events. Usually they are issued in limited quantities for just a short period of time. Unlike regular coins, they are made to be saved not spent. Nevertheless, commemorative coins often have legal-tender status.

During ancient times, the Greeks and Romans would produce commemorative coins to celebrate battle victories. In America, the first gold commemorative coin was struck in 1903 to celebrate the 100th anniversary of the Louisiana Purchase. Two of the most profitable US coins were the 1984 Olympic Eagle (it raised over $74 million dollars to help finance the Los Angeles games) and the 1986 Statue of Liberty Half-Eagle (it brought over $83,000,000 to restore the statue and to benefit the Statue of Liberty/Ellis Island Foundation).

The largest single issue of commemorative gold coins was in 1986 in Japan. Slightly more than nine million coins were minted to commemorate the 60th anniversary of the reign of Emperor Hirohito. These coins weighing 20 grams (almost 2/3 oz T) contained 40,000 yen in gold but had a face value of 100,000 yen, a premium of 150%. There was such a high public demand for the Hirohito coins that another million of them were issued in 1987. Gold prices in 1986 were strengthened as a result of this demand. (From *The Gold Companion* by Timothy Green, p. 32 and *The Investor's Guide to Coin Trading* by Scott Travers, p. 133).

There are private issues of coins as well as governmental ones. The Walt Disney 50th anniversary series coins are particularly attractive in jewelry. Snow White is one of the better known coins of the series. The Walt Disney Doc coin has been a popular purchase for people faced with the dilemma of what can you give a rich doctor who has everything he needs.

Commemorative gold coins make handsome jewelry and souvenir items. However, those that are rare or have high premiums should not be mounted in jewelry. Consult your local coin dealer for recommendations on commemorative coins. A list of the commemorative coins of the US is given below.

**Fig. 11.10** Statue of Liberty coin. Courtesy Wideband Jewelry.

## US Commemorative Gold Coins

| | |
|---|---|
| Louisiana Purchase dollar | 1903 |
| Lewis and Clark Exposition dollar | 1904-1905 |
| Panama Pacific Exposition  $1, $2, $2.50, & $50 | 1915 |
| McKinley Memorial dollar | 1916-1917 |
| Grant Memorial dollar | 1922 |
| US Sesquicentennial  $2.50 | 1926 |
| Art Series (private series) | 1980 |
| Olympic  $10 | 1984 |
| Statue of Liberty  $5 | 1986 |
| Constitution Bicentennial  $5 | 1987 |
| Olympic  $5 | 1988 |
| Congress Bicentennial  $5 | 1989 |
| Mt. Rushmore  $5 | 1991 |
| Olympic  $5 | 1992 |
| Columbus  $5 | 1992 |

The above list is from *Coins* by Margo Russell, page 79 and the 1993 *Standard Catalogue of Coins*.

## Love tokens

Love tokens are currency coins that have been erased and engraved on one side. They were very popular in Europe during the sixteenth century and in the US during the latter part of the nineteenth century.

Jewelers, lonely sailors, soldiers, lovers, etc. would engrave love tokens with initials, messages, or scenes. Some gold coins had initials cut out of other gold coins (often of a different color) and intertwined and soldered onto the base coin. The tokens were made into brooches, bracelets, necklaces, belt buckles and cuff links. According to *Gems and Jewelry Appraising* (p. 151), by Anna Miller, coins with love messages command the top prices, followed by pornographic/erotica, historic, Masonic, and funeral remembrances. If you ever inherit any love tokens from an estate, either an antique dealer or coin dealer may be able to help you determine their value.

## Private and territorial gold coins

The first attempt to create an American gold coin, was perhaps made by a jeweler. In 1787, Ephraim Brasher, a well-known goldsmith and the next-door neighbor of George Washington, produced a trial gold piece. Sometimes referred to as "Brasher's doubloons," these pieces are the most highly prized American coins in existence. Only a few have survived. Even though the Brasher gold pieces were never recognized by any government body, they probably influenced the high quality design of the first official American gold coins. (From *How to Invest in Gold Coins* by Donald Hoppe, pp. 148-149).

During the gold rushes in Georgia and California, bankers, assayers, and private firms struck their own gold coins. It was a lot faster to make the coins near the gold fields than to send the gold back to the government's Philadelphia mint. The unofficial coins were readily accepted by businesses. Today these are among the most valuable US coins, and consequently are not used in jewelry.

Before mounting any rare coin in jewelry, you should first consult a knowledgeable coin dealer or jeweler. He or she can give you an idea of how much the coin is worth before and after mounting. Even though you can get more enjoyment from a coin by wearing it, the possible loss of numismatic value may be so great that you might prefer to select another coin for your jewelry piece. In general, the best place for a rare coin is in a display case or a safe.

As you browse in coin shops, you may notice that some of the coins are sealed in plastic. The coins may have been graded by a coin grading service and afterwards sealed in a clear holder known as a "slab." This is a legitimate way of doing business in the coin trade. Unfortunately, some gem scam victims have assumed that this is also a logical way of buying and selling gems. Clear plastic covers can mask gem flaws and cutting defects. Therefore you should always look at stones outside of their packets or containers before buying them. No legitimate dealer will package a gemstone with the written warning "Breaking the seal will invalidate all guarantees." Even though this is off the subject of this chapter, phony gem investment schemes have become such a critical problem, that they must be mentioned in a consumer jewelry book. Do not buy gems or coins over the phone from people you do not know. Many people have lost their life savings from doing so. Don't become one of them.

If you would like further information about coins, there are lots of helpful books available. Your local coin dealer should be able to recommend some. A few good resource books on gold coins are listed below:

*Gold Coins of the World* by Robert Friedberg.
*Guide to US Coins* by the Editors of Coin World.
*A Guide Book of United States Coins* by R. S. Yeoman.
*How to Invest in Gold Coins* by Donald J Hoppe.
*1993 Standard Catalogue of World Coins* by Chester A Krause, Clifford Mishlor and Colin R. Bruce

# 12

## How Much Is Your Gold Jewelry Worth?

### Estimated Value:  $500

On an insurance appraisal, a statement like this refers to the retail cost of replacing a piece. It does not mean that the owner of the item can resell it for $500. The type of appraisal that gives you the immediate cash value of your jewelry is a liquidation appraisal.  If you are only interested in a verbal estimate of how much you can sell a piece for, there's no point in spending money on an insurance or liquidation appraisal.  The value indicated on an insurance appraisal would be meaningless, and verbal liquidation appraisals are easy to obtain for free.

The least expensive way to find out what your gold jewelry is worth is to ask some gold buyers how much they will give you for it.  It's not hard to find people who buy gold.  They are usually listed in the yellow pages of the phone book under "gold buyers," and they often congregate in jewelry or pawn shop districts.  Signs saying "We buy gold" will help you spot them.  Coin shops or your local jeweler might also buy your gold jewelry.  If you are sincerely interested in selling your jewelry, gold dealers will gladly give you a quote.  They don't like it, though, when people come into their store simply for a free appraisal.

Before you show your gold jewelry to dealers, it's a good idea to calculate its **scrap value** (the value of the materials it's composed of).  In the case of gold jewelry, alloying metals such as silver and copper are not included in the scrap value.  Only the value of the gold is calculated.  To determine the scrap value, you'll need to weigh your jewelry.  If a gold scale or balance is unavailable, try using a postal scale. Despite their limited precision, postal scales can give you a rough estimate of gold weight in grams or in ounces avoirdupois (ounces avoirdupois are used when weighing food, people, letters, etc. Gold weight is measured in ounces troy, which are about 10% heavier).

Real examples are more fun to work with than theoretical ones. In this chapter, the scrap value of a gold bracelet pictured in this book will be calculated. The one chosen is the San Marco bracelet in figure 7.23 of the chapter on gold chains. This bracelet broke two weeks after it was purchased for $120; and the owner, Mrs. Smith, wanted to sell it. Two jewelers said it was not worth repairing because it would probably break again right after it was fixed. The author took the bracelet to some dealers in downtown Los Angeles to see what they would offer for it. The results will be discussed in this chapter.

**Fig. 12.1**   A San Marco chain

The weight of Mrs. Smith's bracelet is **8.2 grams** (5.3  pennyweight). It is **14K**, which means that it is supposed to contain 58.3% gold. To determine the cash value of the gold in the bracelet, we need to know the **spot price of gold**. This is the current cash price at which the major gold exchanges are listing and selling their gold. It's also referred to simply as the **spot gold** or **gold spot**, and it's quoted in terms of the troy ounce.

On the day Mrs. Smith's bracelet was shown to dealers (March 8, 1993), the spot price of gold was **$327.50**. (The financial pages of newspapers or brokerage firms can give you the spot price of gold. In this case, the author checked a display board at a gold exchange in Los Angeles).

The formula below will give us the value of the gold in a 14K gold alloy.

Spot gold  x  gold content (.583) = gold value

$327.50  x .583 = **$190.93**

Since the weight of Mrs. Smith's bracelet is given in grams (or sometimes pennyweight in the US) instead of troy ounces, we need to know how many grams are in one ounce troy. This and other weight equivalencies are given below (**g** = grams, **oz t** = ounce troy, **oz av** = ounce avoirdupois, **dwt** = pennyweight).

| | | | | |
|---|---|---|---|---|
| 1 oz t | = 31.1 g | | 1 dwt | = 0.05 oz t |
| 1 oz t | = 20 dwt | | 1 dwt | = 1.555 g |
| 1 oz t | = 1.097 oz av | | 1 dwt | = 0.055 oz av |
| 1 g | = 0.032 oz t | | 1 oz av | = 0.911 oz t |
| 1 g | = 0.643 dwt | | 1 oz av | = 28.3495 g |
| 1 g | = 0.035 oz av | | 1 oz av | = 18.229 dwt |

Knowing that 1 gram is equivalent to 0.032 oz t, we can calculate the gram price of the gold in the bracelet as follows:

0.032 x $190.93 = **$6.11 per gram**

Mrs. Smith's bracelet weighs 8.2 grams so the gold value of her bracelet is $50.10.

gram weight x gram price = value of gold in bracelet

8.2 g x $6.11 = **$50.10.**

If you don't have a calculator, it will be easier to use rounded figures such as $330 for the spot gold. You can round .583 down to .58 or lower. The results of an assay (test that determines the gold content) of one ounce of 14K gold normally will not be .583. There is always some loss of gold during the assay. In countries such as the US where the use of low karat solder is permitted and where enforcement of the plumb gold law is minimal, the gold may also be underkarated.

One Southern California dealer, who buys a lot of secondhand gold jewelry and has it assayed regularly, finds the 14K gold he buys assays out to 55% gold on the average (Some results are higher, and some lower). Consequently, when he makes an offer on a piece stamped 14K that passes an acid test, he will calculate the gold content as 55%. The average assay results of the 10, 14, and 18k gold he buys is given below along with the equivalent karat value.

| karat stamp | average assay results of one dealer | |
|---|---|---|
| 10K | 38% gold | 9.12 K |
| 14K | 55% gold | 13.20 K |
| 18K | 72% gold | 17.28 K |

If we were to calculate the gold value of the bracelet on the basis of a 55% gold content it would be about $47. Nobody buying it for scrap, though, would pay that amount for it. There are several reasons for this: A profit margin has to be figured into the offer. It costs money to have scrap assayed (tested and separated into its component metals). The piece may contain less gold than expected. If the item turns out to be stolen, it could be seized by the police. In certain areas, dealers must wait a month before they can melt or sell secondhand merchandise. This gives the police time to determine if it's been stolen. Meanwhile the buyer's money is tied up. The higher the buyer's risks, the lower his offer will be.

Mrs. Smith's bracelet was taken to six places that deal in gold. The first was a pawn shop. They said they only loaned money and sold gold jewelry. It's unusual for a pawn shop that deals in gold jewelry to refuse to buy it. One other place said they wouldn't buy the bracelet--a gold exchange which did not deal in jewelry. They recommended an assayer and said they would pay 2% below spot ($327.50) for any gold accompanied by an assay certificate.

The offers of the other four places are listed below. Besides buying gold secondhand, all four places sold gold jewelry.

1. $40
2. $40
3. $30
4. $40, first offer.    $50, second offer after being told $40 was not enough.

It's surprising that three of the four places made the same offer. It seems that in downtown Los Angeles, an offer of about 80% spot is standard in low-risk purchase situations. (It was unlikely this bracelet was stolen or underkarated). This percentage was higher than expected. Perhaps due to high volume and easy access to gold assayers, gold buyers in downtown Los Angeles can offer a higher percentage rate. When selling your gold, keep in mind that the price paid for scrap gold varies considerably depending on the geographic location and market conditions of your area. Naturally, too, it can vary from one gold dealer to another.

All four places weighed the bracelet and checked its karat stamp and trademark. The last buyer was the only one to do an acid test on the bracelet, measure its length, and examine the broken area. He obviously planned to repair it and resell it as a bracelet rather than as scrap. A retail customer might consider a price around $90 to be a bargain. If the bracelet were designed to last, it would be. The $50 is only the value of the gold. It does not include labor, retail profit, import duties (the bracelet was made in Italy), or the cost of the alloying metals of silver and copper. The original purchase price of the machine-made bracelet from a high-volume discount store was $120. It's surprising that it could be resold for $50, 41% of its retail price. More often than not you would receive between 10 to 25% of the current retail price.

Some people become disillusioned with jewelry when they discover how little they can resell it for. This is because they've bought jewelry for the wrong reasons or because a salesperson has misled them about its value. If a store tells you their jewelry is worth double the price they're selling it for, don't believe them. They'd be selling it at the higher price if they could find a willing buyer. Think twice before buying anything from them because if they'll misrepresent the value of their jewelry, there's a chance they'll misrepresent the quality of their gems and gold.

If investment or resale potential is your only reason for purchasing gold jewelry, buy gold bars or coins instead. That way you won't have to pay for labor and retail markups.

When jewelry is bought as a clothing accessory, an ornament, or a memorable gift, it can be a good buy. A solid, well-made piece of jewelry will outlast other accessories. Even today, the gold jewelry and artifacts of the ancient Egyptians look as good as new. When people are asked what gifts they treasure the most, more often than not they'll say jewelry. It's no coincidence that the first official exchange of gifts between a husband and wife are their wedding bands. The wearability and never-ending circular form of the rings make them the perfect symbol of an eternal commitment of love.

Even when a poor jewelry choice is made, it may turn out to be less of a loss than if it were another type of merchandise. Suppose you bought a $120 figurine, and a few weeks later, you wanted to resell it. If the figurine were broken, you probably wouldn't be able to find any buyers for it. In less than 1/2 hour, the author found 3 shops that were willing to pay $40 cash on the spot for Mrs. Smith's broken bracelet. The bracelet could have also been pawned. The pawn value tends to be about 50 to 75% of what the item can be sold for (except in some states where the interest rate allowed decreases as the amount of the loan increases.)

The way in which this chapter calculated the value of Mrs. Smith's bracelet may lead some people to believe that jewelry value equals gold value. Such a conclusion would be wrong. When assessing jewelry, you have to also consider the craftsmanship, the artistic merit, the antique or sentimental value, and the overall desirability of the piece. There is no one answer to the question, "What is your jewelry worth?" The value of a piece depends on the purpose for which it is appraised (insurance, estate, liquidation etc.) and the subjective opinion of the owner or buyer.

## Tips on Reselling Your Jewelry

♦ Have copies available of your purchase receipts, appraisals, and/or lab reports. These help verify the quality and identity of the gems and metals, and they prove you are the rightful owner. The lower the buyers' risk, the more they will be willing to offer.

♦ Try taking the jewelry back to the store where you bought it. Ask if they will buy it back or offer you credit towards other jewelry. Sometimes the original seller will give you the best offer.

♦ Consider having a jewelry store sell your piece on consignment. Consignment sales sometimes bring the highest price.

♦ Get offers from people who understand the value of your jewelry. An antique dealer, for example, will probably have the greatest appreciation for the antique value of a piece. A coin dealer will be the most likely to know the value of a coin pendant. Colored stone experts will offer more for a valuable ruby or emerald than a pawnbroker who doesn't understand how they are valued. In fact, there are a few pawnbrokers who won't give you anything for colored stones. They'll only pay for gold and diamonds. There are others, however, who are very knowledgeable about colored gems and who will offer you a fair price for them.

♦ Get offers from people who sell jewelry like yours at the retail level. The best offer for Mrs. Smith's bracelet was from a retail jeweler who sold and repaired gold chains. The retail jewelry value is higher than the wholesale or scrap value of a piece.

♦ Do not invite strangers to your house to look at jewelry. This could result in a hold-up or burglary. If you need to show your jewelry to a buyer you don't know, have him or her meet you inside a bank where you can take it out of a safe deposit box. Even this procedure can be risky.

♦ Do not appear to be desperate for money, even if you are. Usually the more eager you are to sell, the less the buyer will offer.

# 13

## Caring for Your Gold Jewelry

**W**hich of the following scratches most easily?

♦ Glass
♦ A sea shell
♦ Pure gold
♦ Pure silver

Since pure gold is the softest, it's the easiest to scratch. Glass can be from 5 to 100 times harder than gold. A sea shell is about 3 to 4 times harder, and silver is slightly harder than gold. This means that if you place gold jewelry in a box on top of other pieces, it's almost sure to get scratched. Therefore, when you store jewelry, place each piece in a separate pouch or plastic bag, or wrap them individually in soft material. Padded jewelry bags with lots of pockets are also handy for storing jewelry.

### Cleaning Gold Mountings

Brushes can scratch gold too. Therefore, you should avoid using them to clean it. Instead use a soft cloth to rub dirt off the metal. The safest cleaning solution for gold jewelry is warm water with a mild liquid detergent. Never boil jewelry. This can cause the stones to crack or change color.

Jewelers also like to use sudsy ammonia. It's safe to use on gold, but it can damage stones such as pearls. Avoid cleaning gold with toothpaste, powder cleansers or scouring pads because these can wear away the metal.

Since jewelry gold is not pure, a variety of chemical products may discolor or dissolve it. A few of these products and their affect on gold alloys are as follows:

157

♦ **Chlorine**--it can pit and dissolve the metal, causing prongs to snap and mountings to break apart. Afterwards, it might appear as if you've been sold defective or fake gold jewelry. Therefore, avoid wearing gold jewelry in swimming pools or hot tubs that have chlorine disinfectants, and never soak it or clean it with bleach.

♦ **Lotions and cosmetics**--besides leaving a film on the jewelry piece, they may tarnish it, especially if it's made of 10K gold. If possible, put your jewelry on last, after applying make-up and spraying your hair.

♦ **Perm solutions**--they have a tendency to turn 10K gold and low-karat solder joints dark brown or black.

♦ **Some medications**--they may cause a chemical reaction in certain people. This can make their skin turn black when it comes into contact with the gold alloy.

♦ **Polishing compounds**--They can blacken your skin if they remain on the gold. Polishing cloths sold in jewelry stores may contain a mild abrasive for shining the metal. When using these cloths, be sure to wash or wipe the metal thoroughly afterwards.

## Other Tips

♦ If possible, avoid wearing jewelry while participating in contact sports or doing housework, gardening, repairs, etc. The mounting can be damaged, and stones can be chipped, scratched and cracked. If during rough work, you want to wear a ring for sentimental reasons or to avoid losing it, wear protective gloves. Hopefully, your ring has a smooth setting style with no high prongs.

♦ When you set jewelry near a sink, make sure the drains are plugged or that it's put in a protective container. Otherwise, don't take the jewelry off.

♦ Clean your jewelry on a regular basis. Then you won't have to use risky procedures to clean it later on.

♦ Occasionally check your jewelry for loose stones. Shake it or tap it lightly with your forefinger while holding it next to your ear. If you hear the stones rattle or click, have a jeweler tighten the prongs.

♦ Avoid exposing your jewelry to sudden changes of temperature. If you wear it in a hot tub and then go in cold water with it on, the stones could crack or shatter. Also keep jewelry away from steam and hot pots and ovens in the kitchen.

♦ Take a photo of your jewelry (a macro lens is helpful). Just lay it all together on a table for the photo. If the jewelry is ever lost or stolen, you'll have documentation to help you remember and prove what you had.

♦ About every six months, have a jewelry professional check your ring for loose stones or wear on the mounting. Many jewelers will do this free of charge, and they'll be happy to answer your questions regarding the care of your jewelry.

# Quiz (Chapters 10, 11, 12, & 13)

## True or False?

1. The grape-leaf motif is what distinguishes Black Hills gold jewelry from other types.

2. A good and easy way to clean gold jewelry is to spread toothpaste on it and rub it clean with a brush.

3. Adding copper to gold makes it pinker. Adding silver makes it greener and paler.

4. An ideal way of displaying a very rare coin is to mount it in jewelry.

5. In terms of actual gold value, a chain weighing 6 pennyweight is worth more than one weighing 6 grams.

6. It's okay to go swimming while wearing gold jewelry as long as the piece(s) doesn't contain any delicate gems such as pearls.

7. The main coloring agent for white gold is nickel.

8. The one-ounce American Eagle contains less gold than the one-ounce Canadian Maple Leaf. (The American gold bullion coin is 22K whereas the Canadian one is 24K.)

9. If a 12K gold necklace weighs one ounce on a postal scale, and the spot price of gold is $400 an ounce. Then the gold value of the necklace would be $200.

10. Before reselling jewelry, it's a good idea to get a written appraisal from someone who will give it the highest possible value.

## Answers:

1.   T

2.   F     The toothpaste would act as an abrasive, and the brush could scratch the metal.

3.   T

4.   F     You could diminish its value considerably by wearing it in jewelry. Always consult a knowledgeable coin dealer or jeweler before mounting coins in jewelry.

5.   T

6.   F     The chlorine in the pool can eat away at the gold causing it to pit and gradually dissolve.

7.   T

8.   F     One-ounce bullion coins contain one ounce of gold no matter what their karat value may be. The one-ounce refers to the weight of the gold in the coin, not the weight of the coin. A one-ounce American Eagle coin weighs more than a one-ounce Canadian Maple Leaf.

9.   F     It would be worth about 10% less, because the one ounce avoirdupois of a postal scale only equals 0.911 ounce troy, the unit of weight for gold.

10.  F     Such an appraisal would be a waste of money because it would be ignored by secondhand buyers. Documentation regarding the weight, quality, and identity of your gems and precious metals could be helpful, though.

      When an appraiser gives your jewelry an inflated value, he/she is doing you a disservice. If it's for insurance, you can end up paying an unnecessarily high premium. If it's for other reasons, the inflated value can make the whole document suspect and therefore of little value to you.

# 14

# Finding a Good Buy

Ed wants to buy his wife, Adelia, a diamond anniversary band for their 25th anniversary. They've both read *The Gold Jewelry Buying Guide* and are aware that they'll need some expert help in selecting a well-crafted ring. As they shop, they discover that even when salespeople are knowledgeable about diamonds, they may know little about jewelry craftsmanship.

Freddie, the owner of a small jewelry store, is an exception. He asks Adelia if she plans to wear the ring all the time. When she says yes, he tells her she'll need something sturdy. Adelia wants a channel setting, so he takes out a few styles for her to try on.

Adelia finds two she likes with lots of sparkle and brilliance. Freddie has her look at both of them under the microscope to examine the diamonds and the mounting. There are no cracks, chips, or big flaws in any of the diamonds. However, the diamonds in one ring have more little white flaws than those in the other one. Freddie then points out the superior setting and structural quality of the ring with more diamond flaws. On Freddie's advice, Adelia and Ed decide to get this ring. This is an easy sale for Freddie, and it's a pleasant experience for Adelia and Ed. They've gotten sound, professional advice and a ring they can be proud of.

Betty is looking for a gold chain that she can wear with or without a pendant. After reading *The Gold Jewelry Buying Guide*, she's decided that a rope or link chain would be best for her. The first question that some of the salespeople ask is how much she wants to spend.

One salesman, named Reed, seems to be more focused on helping her find a good chain than in claiming his prices are the best in town. He asks her to look in his showcase and pick out an example of the type and size of pendant she wants to hang on it. Then he shows her some chains that would compliment it and be strong enough to hold it. Betty sees two that she likes. Reed then has her try on the chains with the pendant to see how they feel and how the pendant rolls on the chain. She ends up buying a style of link chain that she hasn't seen elsewhere. Not only will it hold her pendant securely, it will also look attractive worn by itself. Betty is pleased both with the chain and the expert help she's received from Reed.

Lydia wants to buy her husband, Al, something made of gold for his 50th birthday. Al doesn't wear jewelry. After seeing a nugget watch and some of the custom-made pieces in *The Gold Jewelry Buying Guide*, an idea comes to her. She'll get Al a custom-designed gold watch. He's an avid traveler, so she'll choose a couple slides he's taken of two of his favorite places. Then she'll have her jeweler, Mr. Norton, reproduce the miniature scenes on either side of the watch.

Mr. Norton, who is known for his creative designs, likes the idea and suggests including Al's birthstone. So Lydia goes through her husband's slides, picks out two, and reminisces about the good times they've had together on trips. After Mr. Norton finishes the wax models of the two scenes, he has Lydia check them over. She tells him they look fine and to proceed.

The watch turns out better than Lydia expected. Al can't believe his eyes when he opens the package. He loves the watch and this makes Lydia feel good. She would have never thought that buying a birthday present could be so much fun.

Shopping for gold jewelry turned out to be a positive experience for Lydia, Betty, and Adelia & Ed. This was because they took time beforehand to learn some buying tips. Also, they dealt with competent salespeople. Listed below are some guidelines to help make your shopping experience a positive one, too.

**Note if the jeweler talks about quality.** Jewelers who only promote their price and their styles may not have quality merchandise.

**Look at the back of the mounting.** A good finish and polish throughout the piece is a sign of good craftsmanship.

**If the jewelry contains gemstones, make sure there is metal securing the stones in their settings.** Count the prongs. One or two prongs is not enough to hold a round stone securely.

**If you are having jewelry custom-made, repaired, or sized, specify that you want the appropriate solder used** (for example 14K solder on 14K gold). The use of a lower-karat solder could cause your skin to blacken or the solder joints to turn dark brown or green. It would also lower the overall karat value of your piece.

**Ask if the piece is hollow or solid.** Light-weight, hollow mountings are ideal for earrings, but they're not a wise choice for an everyday ring. If you're buying a hollow bracelet, ask the store if you can try denting it with gentle finger-tip pressure. If the salesperson says no, then don't buy it. Bracelets that dent easily won't last long with the knocking and scraping they'll undergo while worn on the wrist.

**It there's a clasp, verify that it works**. Try to open and close it by yourself a couple times. Listen for the click, then pull on the clasp gently to see if it comes undone or remains secure.

**Specify that you want jewelry which will last.** When salespeople see that you are interested in well-made jewelry, they are more likely to show you their better pieces.

**Check to see if there is a karat stamp and trademark on the piece.** Even though they are not necessarily a guarantee that the gold content is as marked, they are an indication. If you ever decide to resell the piece later on, these marks would be important.

**Try on the piece and walk around with it.** Then answer the following questions. If the piece is a good choice, all your answers will be positive.

- ◆ **Does it look good on you?**
- ◆ **Does it feel comfortable?**
- ◆ **Is there a good chance it will stay in style?**
- ◆ **Have rough edges been polished away?**
- ◆ **Does it look sturdy enough for the purpose for which you plan to wear it?**

The above guidelines provide a base from which you can learn how to evaluate gold jewelry. Besides helping you compare prices, knowing how to judge jewelry quality will help you get lifetime enjoyment from your jewelry. How can you appreciate its craftsmanship and beauty if you don't know anything about it except for its price, weight and karat quality?

Consider, for example, the bird brooch in figure 14.1 and color photo 10A. If you only knew that it was cast from 9K gold, you'd probably think of it as just an ordinary brooch.

**Fig. 14.1** A Scottish-made brooch. *Photo courtesy of the designer, Alan Hodgkinson.*

Suppose, however, you're also given the following information:

♦ The coloring and design of the bird brooch matches the bird it represents--the fieldfare, a European thrush.

♦ The goldsmith created the coloring by heating the gold brooch till it turned black through oxidation. Afterwards, with special scraping and cutting techniques, he took the metal back down to dark-brown, brown, orange, coppery orange, and yellow gold, the original color. The white nape and feathers of the bird were plated with rhodium (a white metal) and then scraped back down to expose more subtle shades of white. If the piece had been made in 18K gold, this wide range of colors could not have been produced. The high percentage of alloying metals in 9K gold allows it to turn black when heated to a certain temperature.

♦ The finishing techniques were done entirely by hand.

♦ This is an original, one-of-a-kind piece.

♦ The bird was a gift for an ornithologist, whose favorite bird is the fieldfare. One of the designer's hobbies is bird-watching.

♦ The occasion for the gift was a 40th wedding anniversary, represented by the ruby. Fieldfares feed on red berries so ruby beads complete with blackened gold calyx were an appropriate accent for the brooch (the calyx is the external leafy part of a flower).

With this added information, it's easy to understand that this is a very special, valuable brooch. When you look at this piece under magnification, you gain further appreciation for its craftsmanship and the attention paid to detail.

As you shop, you'll find there is a variety of types of gold jewelry to chose from--mass-produced, custom-made; low-priced, high-priced; 10-karat, 18-karat; machine-made, hand-fabricated. Any of these types can be of high quality. Any of these types can be of low quality. There's only one sure way of determining the quality of a piece and that's to look at it.

But to spot good quality, you have to know something about jewelry craftsmanship. To help increase your knowledge, whenever you're in a jewelry store, ask the salesperson to show you some examples of well-crafted merchandise. Then have him or her explain to you what makes it high quality. Whenever possible, look at the jewelry under magnification. This will help you see details not visible to the naked eye and it will increase your powers of observation. Examine the jewelry that you own and determine which has given you the most wear and the most pleasure. Gradually you'll learn to recognize good value. And this will enable you to select jewelry that you'll treasure throughout your life.

# Bibliography

## Books

Allen, Gina. *Gold!* New York: Thomas Y. Crowell, 1064.

Bovin, Murray. *Jewelry Making.* Forest Hills, NY: Bovin Publishing, 1967.

Branson, Oscar T. *What You Need to Know About Your Gold and Silver.* Tucson, AZ: Treasure Chest Publications, 1980.

Brod, I. Jack. *Consumer's Guide to Buying and Selling Gold, Silver, and Diamonds.* Garden City, NY: Doubleday, 1985.

Burkett, Russell. *Everything You Wanted to Know about Gold and Other Precious Metals.* Whittier, CA: Gem Guides Book Co., 1975.

Cavelti, Peter C. *How to Invest in Gold.* Chicago: Follett Publishing Company. 1979.

Cavelti, Peter C. *New Profits in Gold, Silver & Strategic Metals.* New York: McGraw-Hill, 1985.

Consumer Guide. *Coin Finder.* Skokie, IL: Consumer Guide.

Dawson. *Goldsmiths and Silversmiths' Work.* New York: G. P. Putnams's Sons, 1907.

Edwards, Rod. *The Technique of Jewelry.* New York: Charles Scribner's Sons, 1977.

Gemological Institute of America. Appraisal Seminar handbook.

Gemological Institute of America. Jewelry Repair Workbook.

Gemological Institute of America. Jewelry Sales Course.

Goldemberg, Rose Leiman. *Antique Jewelry: a Practical and Passionate Guide.* New York: Crown Publishing Co., 1976.

Green, Timothy. *The Gold Companion.* London: Rosendale Press, 1991.

Gould, Maurice M. *Gould's Gold and Silver Guide to Coins.*

Hoppe, Donald J. *How to Invest in Gold Coins.* Rochelle, NY: Arlington House. 1970.

Krause, Chester L., Clifford Mishler, & Colin R. Bruce. *1993 Standard Catalogue of World Coins.* Iola, Wisconsin: Krause Publications, 1993.

Jarvis, Charles A. *Jewelry Manufacture and Repair.* New York: Bonanza, 1979.

Marcum, David. *Fine Gems and Jewelry.* Homewood, IL.: Dow Jones-Irwin, 1986.

Merton, Henry A. *Your Gold & Silver.* New York: Macmillan, 1981.

Miller, Anna M. *Gems and Jewelry Appraising.* New York: Van Nostrand Reinhold, 1988.

Miller, Anna M. *Illustrated Guide to Jewelry Appraising.* New York: Van Nostrand Reinhold, 1990.

Morton, Philip. *Contemporary Jewelry.* New York: Holt, Rinehart, and Winston, 1976.

Preston, William S. *Guides for the Jewelry Industry.* New York: Jewelers Vigilance Committee, Inc., 1986.

Revere, Alan, *Professional Goldsmithing.* New York: Van Nostrand Reinhold, 1991.

Richards, Alison. *Handmade Jewelry.* New York: Funk & Wagnalls. 1976.

Russell, Margo. *Coins.* Philadelpia: Running Press. 1989.

Sarett, Morton R. *The Jewelry in Your Life.* Chicago: Nelson-Hall, 1979.

Schumann, Walter. *Gemstones of the World.* New York: Sterling 1977.

Smith, Ernest. *Working in Precious Metals.* Colchester, England: N. A. G. Press Ltd. 1933.

Sprintzen, Alice. *Jewelry: Basic Techniques and Design.* Radnor, PA: Chilton, 1980

Sutherland, C. H. V. *Gold: Its Beauty, Power and Allure.* New York: McGraw-Hill, 1969.

Travers, Scott A. *The Investor's Guide to Coin Trading.* New York: John Wiley & Sons, 1990.

Untracht, Oppi. *Jewelry Concepts & Technology.* New York: Doubleday, 1982.

Von Neumann, Robert. *The Design and Creation of Jewelry.* Radnor, PA: Chilton, 1972.

Wolenik, Robert Irwin. *The Coinage Guide.* New York: Simon & Schuster, 1987.

Wykoff, Gerald L. *Beyond the Glitter.* Washington DC: Adamas, 1982.

Yeoman, R. S. *A Guide Book of United States Coins, 46th Edition, 1993.* Racine, WI: Western Publishing Co., 1992

## Magazines

*American Jewelry Manufacturer.* Philadelphia, PA.

*Gems and Gemology.* Santa Monica, CA: Gemological Institute of America.

*The Goldsmith.* Atlanta, GA: Allen/Abernethy Division of A/S/M Communications Inc.

*Jewelers Circular Keystone.* Radnor, PA: Chilton Publishing Co.

*Jewelers' Quarterly Magazine.* Sonoma, CA.

*Modern Jeweler.* Lincolnshire, IL: Vance Publishing Inc.

*National Jeweler.* New York: Gralla Publications.

## Miscellaneous   (Articles, Catalogues, Brochures, etc.)

Canadian Placer Gold Sales Limited.  Informational Letter.  Vancouver, British Columbia. (1993)

Consumer and Corporate Affairs Canada.  "A Guide to the Precious Metals Marking Act and Regulations."

Federman, David.  "Electroforming: Big, bold and light." *Modern Jeweler*, p. 65-66, January, 1993.

GIA and the World Gold Council.  The Gold Seminar handbook.

Johnson Matthey, "Platinum Jewelry Products."

Mercer, Meredith E.  "Methods for Determining the Gold Content of Jewelry Metals." *Gems & Gemology,* p. 222-233, Winter 1992.

Platinum Guild International.  "Talking Platinum."

Reactive Metals Studio Inc.  1993 Catalogue.  Clarkdale, Az.

Rio Grande Albuquerque.  "Tools."

River Gems & Findings Catalogue.

World Gold Council. *Jewelry Market Report*.  New York, Spring/Summer 1991.

Stuller. "The Findings Book."

Swest Inc.  "Jewelers' Findings & Stones & Metals"

# Index

# Order Form

To:   International Jewelry Publications
P.O. Box 13384
Los Angeles, CA 90013-0384  USA

Please send me:

\_\_\_\_ copies of **THE GOLD JEWELRY BUYING GUIDE**
Within California $21.60 each (includes sales tax)    _____
All other destinations $19.95 US each    _____

\_\_\_\_ copies of **THE RUBY & SAPPHIRE BUYING GUIDE.**
Within California $21.60 each (includes sales tax)    _____
All other destinations $19.95 US each    _____

\_\_\_\_ copies of **THE PEARL BUYING GUIDE**
Within California $20.51 each (includes sales tax)    _____
All other destinations $18.95 US each    _____

\_\_\_\_ copies of **THE DIAMOND RING BUYING GUIDE.**
Within California $14.02 each (includes sales tax)    _____
All other destinations $12.95 US each    _____

**Postage & Handling for Books**

USA:  first book $1.50, each additional copy $.75    _____
Canada & foreign - surface mail:  first book $2.50, ea. addl. $1.50    _____
Canada & Mexico - airmail:  first book $3.75, ea. addl. $2.50    _____
All other foreign destinations - airmail:  first book $9.00, ea. addl. $5.00    _____

\_\_\_\_ copies of **DIAMONDS: FASCINATING FACTS.**
Within California $4.28 each (includes sales tax)    _____
All other destinations $3.95 US each    _____

**Postage for Diamonds: Fascinating Facts**
USA:  $0.55 per booklet    _____
Canada & Mexico - airmail:  $0.80 per booklet    _____
All other foreign destinations - airmail:  $1.25 per booklet    _____

## Total Amount Enclosed    _____
(USA funds drawn on a USA bank)

Ship to:

Name_____

Address_____

City_____ State or Province_____

Postal or Zip Code_____ Country _____

# OTHER PUBLICATIONS BY RENEE NEWMAN

## The Ruby & Sapphire Buying Guide: How to Spot Value & Avoid Ripoffs

A guide to buying, evaluating, identifying, and caring for rubies and sapphires.

Discover:

* How to choose a good-quality stone
* How to tell a fake from a real ruby or sapphire
* How to compare prices and save money
* How to buy gems abroad

"**Solid, informative and comprehensive** . . . dissects each aspect of ruby and sapphire value in detail and quizzes the reader on key points at the end of each chapter. . . a wealth of grading information . . . *The Ruby & Sapphire Buying Guide* is a definite thumbs-up for both the unskilled and semiskilled buyer and seller. There is something here for everyone."
 C. R. Beesley, President, American Gemological Laboratories, New York. *Jewelers' Circular Keystone*

"**Highly recommended** . . . includes a great deal of gemmological as well as commercial information; text photographs are clear and cover many situations for appraisal which have rarely been put forward in gemmology texts before. . . . useful to the gemmology student as well as to the dealer or purchaser of jewelry."
 *The Journal of Gemmology*, a publication of the Gemmological Association of Great Britain

"**Well-written**--not so technical that you would need a dictionary to understand what is written and, most important, the information in it is all pertinent to anyone who wants to buy and sell colored gemstones. I have recommended this book to all my students and I enthusiastically recommend it to anyone interested in colored gemstones. Well done!"
 H. B. Leith, teacher-gemologist, master goldsmith

204 pages, 10 color and 86 black/white photos, 7" by 9", $19.95 US.

**AVAILABLE AT** bookstores, jewelry supply stores, the GIA, through the Jewelers' Book Club and *Lapidary Journal* or by mail: See reverse side for order form.

## Diamonds: Fascinating Facts

**An informative booklet** with entertaining facts, poems, and statistics about diamonds.

**A novel and appropriate greeting card to include with a diamond gift.** It comes with a 6" x 9" white envelope. The inside front cover is designed to allow for a personal message.

Full-color, 16-page, self-cover booklet with six 5" x 7 1/2" photos, $3.95 US.

# The Pearl Buying Guide

This informative book explains and shows:

* How to judge pearl quality
* How imitation pearls differ from those that are real
* How cultured pearls differ from those that are natural
* How South Sea, freshwater, and Japanese saltwater pearls are valued
* How a simple pearl necklace can be a versatile piece of jewelry

**An easily read, interesting, and helpful book on pearls.** A guide for a pearl buying customer who wants to make an intelligent purchase... a good starting place for a jewelry clerk wanting to improve his or her salesmanship and would even be a help for a graduate gemologist seeking a better understanding of what to look for when examining or appraising a pearl necklace.
*The Canadian Gemmologist*, a publication of The Canadian Gemmological Association

**An interesting and easy-to-understand guide** to buying, evaluating, selecting, and caring for pearls and pearl jewelry. The many photographs are valuable in illustrating the characteristics of and differences among pearls. Overall, the guide is useful to all types of readers, from the professional jeweler to the average patron...
*Library Journal*

186 pages, 7" X 9", 8 color and 90 black & white photos, $18.95 US

# The Diamond Ring Buying Guide:
# How to Spot Value & Avoid Ripoffs

Find out:

* How to judge diamond quality
* How to detect diamond imitations
* How to select a ring style that's both practical and flattering
* How to compare the prices of diamonds and jewelry mountings

**"Filled with useful information, drawings, pictures, and short quizzes.** . . presents helpful suggestions on detecting diamond imitations, in addition to well-though-out discussions of diamond cutting, and how the various factors can influence value . . . a very readable way for the first-time diamond buyer to get acquainted with the often intimidating subject of purchasing a diamond."
Stephen C. Hofer, President, Colored Diamond Laboratory Services, *Jewelers' Circular Keystone*

151 pages, 85 black and white photos, 7" by 9", $12.95 US

**AVAILABLE AT** bookstores, jewelry supply stores, through the GIA and *the Lapidary Journal* & Jeweler's Book Clubs or by mail: See reverse side for order form.

# Order Form

To:    International Jewelry Publications
P.O. Box 13384
Los Angeles, CA 90013-0384  USA

Please send me:

____ copies of **THE GOLD JEWELRY BUYING GUIDE**
Within California $21.60 each (includes sales tax)
All other destinations $19.95 US each

____ copies of **THE RUBY & SAPPHIRE BUYING GUIDE.**
Within California $21.60 each (includes sales tax)
All other destinations $19.95 US each

____ copies of **THE PEARL BUYING GUIDE**
Within California $20.51 each (includes sales tax)
All other destinations $18.95 US each

____ copies of **THE DIAMOND RING BUYING GUIDE.**
Within California $14.02 each (includes sales tax)
All other destinations $12.95 US each

**Postage & Handling for Books**

USA:  first book $1.50, each additional copy $.75
Canada & foreign - surface mail:  first book $2.50, ea. addl. $1.50
Canada & Mexico - airmail:  first book $3.75, ea. addl. $2.50
All other foreign destinations - airmail:  first book $9.00, ea. addl. $5.00

____ copies of **DIAMONDS: FASCINATING FACTS.**
Within California $4.28 each (includes sales tax)
All other destinations $3.95 US each

**Postage for Diamonds: Fascinating Facts**
USA:  $0.55 per booklet
Canada & Mexico - airmail:  $0.80 per booklet
All other foreign destinations - airmail:  $1.25 per booklet

## Total Amount Enclosed
(USA funds drawn on a USA bank)

---

Ship to:

Name_____

Address_____

City_____ State or Province_____

Postal or Zip Code_____ Country _____